Gender Ideologies and Military Labor Markets in the US

Gender Ideologies and Military Labor Markets in the US offers a comprehensive analysis of the relationship between changes in military gender ideologies and structural changes in US military and society.

By investigating how social and military changes have influenced gender ideologies, the author develops an approach that (re)connects military gender ideologies to the social conditions of their production and distribution, and explains their transformation as effects of changing social and political relations and conflicts. Examining the role of different groups of social actors, media debates on women's military participation, and gender ideologies inherent in depictions of military women, the author seeks to contextualize these ideologies within structural change in the US military and society, relating them to the gender-specific division of labor on civilian and military labor markets.

This work provides a deeper understanding of the nexus between military re-structuring processes, women's military integration, and changes of gender ideologies in regard to war and the military, and will be of great interest to students and scholars of gender, security studies, and US politics.

Saskia Stachowitsch is a post-doctorate Researcher in the Department of Politics, University of Vienna, Austria.

Routledge Studies in US Foreign Policy

Edited by Inderjeet Parmar,
University of Manchester
and John Dumbrell,
University of Durham

This new series sets out to publish high-quality works by leading and emerging scholars critically engaging with United States Foreign Policy. The series welcomes a variety of approaches to the subject and draws on scholarship from international relations, security studies, international political economy, foreign policy analysis and contemporary international history.

Subjects covered include the role of administrations and institutions, the media, think tanks, ideologues and intellectuals, elites, transnational corporations, public opinion, and pressure groups in shaping foreign policy, US relations with individual nations, with global regions and global institutions and America's evolving strategic and military policies.

The series aims to provide a range of books – from individual research monographs and edited collections to textbooks and supplemental reading for scholars, researchers, policy analysts, and students.

United States Foreign Policy and National Identity in the 21st Century
Edited by Kenneth Christie

New Directions in US Foreign Policy
Edited by Inderjeet Parmar, Linda B. Miller and Mark Ledwidge

America's "Special Relationships"
Foreign and domestic aspects of the politics of alliance
Edited by John Dumbrell and Axel R. Schäfer

US Foreign Policy in Context
National ideology from the founders to the Bush doctrine
Adam Quinn

The United States and NATO since 9/11
The transatlantic alliance renewed
Ellen Hallams

Soft Power and US Foreign Policy
Theoretical, historical and contemporary perspectives
Edited by Inderjeet Parmar and Michael Cox

The US Public and American Foreign Policy
Edited by Andrew Johnstone and Helen Laville

American Foreign Policy and Postwar Reconstruction
Comparing Japan and Iraq
Jeff Bridoux

Neoconservatism and American Foreign Policy
A critical analysis
Danny Cooper

US Policy Towards Cuba
Since the Cold War
Jessica F. Gibbs

Constructing US Foreign Policy
The curious case of Cuba
David Bernell

Race and US Foreign Policy
The African-American foreign affairs network
Mark Ledwidge

Gender Ideologies and Military Labor Markets in the US
Saskia Stachowitsch

Gender Ideologies and Military Labor Markets in the US

Saskia Stachowitsch

Routledge
Taylor & Francis Group

LONDON AND NEW YORK

First published 2012
by Routledge
2 Park Square, Milton Park, Abingdon, Oxon OX14 4RN

Simultaneously published in the USA and Canada
by Routledge
711 Third Avenue, New York, NY 10017

Routledge is an imprint of the Taylor & Francis Group, an informa business

British Library Cataloguing in Publication Data
A catalogue record for this book is available from the British Library

Library of Congress Cataloging in Publication Data
Stachowitsch, Saskia.
Gender ideologies and military labor markets in the U.S./Saskia
Stachowitsch.
    p. cm.—(Routledge studies in US foreign policy)
Includes bibliographical references and index.
1. Women and the military—United States.   2. United States—
Armed Forces—Women.   3. United States—Armed Forces—
Reorganization.   4. Sociology, Military—United States.   I. Title.
UB418.W65S725 2011
331.4'8135500973—dc22

                                                        2011008768

ISBN: 978-0-415-66707-4 (hbk)
ISBN: 978-0-203-80468-1 (ebk)

Typeset in Times New Roman
by RefineCatch Limited, Bungay, Suffolk

MIX
Paper from
responsible sources
FSC
www.fsc.org   FSC® C004839

Printed and bound in Great Britain by the MPG Books Group

Contents

List of tables and figures

Tables

Figure

Acknowledgments

Without the support, advice, insights, and encouragement of the following people, this book would never have been written. First and foremost, Eva Kreisky has inspired my interest in the subject and guided me through the research process. In addition to her helpful criticism and feedback, she has encouraged me to think beyond narrow disciplinary confines, for which I convey my deepest gratitude. Michael Stachowitsch has contributed immensely to the quality of the text and offered not only linguistic expertise, but perspectives and ideas from a different field of academic inquiry. I thank him for his enormous effort and insightful comments. I also thank Christoph Clar who supported me in this project from start to finish and deserves a great deal of credit for anything accomplished here.

1   Introduction

The following question was sent to *The Washington Post*'s "Miss Manners," and answered in her column in 1989:

> Q) I am a lieutenant in the US Navy and an unmarried woman. Military officers frequently have official functions to attend which entail formal uniforms and many traditional toasts, and all officers present are expected to join in the toasts. One of these toasts is usually, "To our charming ladies," and is directed by the masculine toaster to the wives and lady friends present. Whether I attend these functions with a date or not, I am left in a quandary. Should I stand and toast my escort, should he stand and toast me, or should we both sit quietly? If I don't join the toast, I'm not taking part, and I don't feel it appropriate to allow myself to be classified as one of the charming escorts, since I am at the occasion in an official capacity. Yet neither do I feel I should toast my escort as a "charming lady." No one else at these functions seems to know what to do.
>
> A) Time for a major updating in the Navy. Miss Manners hopes all personnel are paying attention. Of course this is an impossible situation for you. You are both an officer and a lady, and to pretend you are either one and not the other on an occasion when both are present would be ridiculous. This custom only made sense when all officers were gentlemen and their guests all ladies. Henceforth, Miss Manners unilaterally declares that the toast should be "To our charming guests."
>
> (Martin 1989)

Despite its comic effects, that "Miss Manners" column basically treats the same subject as the study at hand: the change of military gender ideologies in the face of women's integration into the Armed Forces. Question and answer both suggest that the situation of US military women and their perception have changed during the last decades and that traditional gender ideologies have partly become anachronistic in the course of institutional modernization. In the US, the debate on women's roles in military institutions has been long, arduous, and ongoing. Today, the issue is no longer whether women should be eligible to join the Armed Forces but whether their integration should remain restricted and to what extent.

The media has been one of the main arenas in which these issues have been fiercely debated. Within media discourses on gender integration, different images of military women and perceptions of femininity and masculinity have been promoted to argue for or against integration policies. This study aims at making sense of these gender ideologies and their continuities and discontinuities. It involves examining the structural transformations in US military and society and relating shifts in gender ideologies to the gender-specific division of labor on civilian and military labor markets.

(Re)uniting the material and the cultural

The relations between gender and warfare have attracted increasing academic attention from the social sciences since the 1980s. Research on women's integration into military institutions has been an important issue within this field of study. The focus so far has mostly been either on structural and institutional change in military organizations, or on cultural constructions, identities, and symbolic representations of gender in regard to the military and violent conflict. "Structural" approaches have mostly depicted cultural and ideological aspects as one of many groups of factors—one often considered less influential than strategic or technological aspects (Segal 1995; Iskra *et al.* 2002). "Cultural" approaches, in contrast, have included structural factors only as vaguely defined contexts (Peach 1996; Titunik 2008). In most cases, both of these approaches have not systematically related structural and cultural dimensions of social phenomena to each other in the analysis. In this sense, gender and military research has suffered from a disconnection between structural and cultural perspectives, a condition that Nancy Fraser (2004) has pointed out for gender theory and research in general. This dualism needs to be overcome. It calls for a social and political science approach that (re)connects military gender ideologies to the social conditions of their production and distribution and that explains their transformation in relation to changing social and political relations and conflicts.

Accordingly, gender must be conceptualized as a social phenomenon that is effective on different levels of social reality. As a structural category, gender organizes social relations and positions men and women differently within social structures and institutions. These patterns of inclusion and exclusion correspond to ideologies of a "natural" gender order including ideals of masculinity and femininity. Gender ideologies relate to historically and culturally varying forms of gender-specific division of labor that are constantly contested. Gender ideologies concerning war and the military therefore depend on gender-specific inclusion in and exclusion from military institutions and labor markets. Under the conditions of military restructuring and increased gender integration, traditional gender ideologies are weakened in some areas, while they remain functional in others, e.g. in ground combat. Their functionality is defined by the changing social and military conditions under which they are produced and transformed.

To investigate the relations between changing structural conditions and gender ideologies, different theoretical approaches to the social embeddedness of cultural and ideological phenomena are available (see Chapter 2). Analyzing both military institutions and military ideology calls for giving equal consideration to the material and the ideological side of the equation. The appropriate research strategy is an undogmatic materialist approach, one that claims that (1) the material conditions of social life have a dominant influence on changes in social systems and (2) the causes of social change lie predominantly in the mode of production and reproduction, in the division of labor, and in the institutionally and structurally determined power relations. These material relations must therefore be incorporated in the analysis of values, norms, and ideologies. At the same time, the role of these cultural aspects in social and military change needs to be acknowledged.

Materialist research strategies have often been criticized for their alleged economistic reductionism and determinism. To avoid these traps, a key research focus must be the *reciprocity* between social, military and ideological change. The following chapters identify the influence of social structures, institutions, modes of labor division, and socio-economic relations on military gender ideologies. Nonetheless, ideology is not considered a mere side effect of material relations. Rather, it is an important factor in the complex and conflictual processes of social change. Military gender ideologies reflect the demographic, technological, social, economic, and political conditions of military gender integration, the organization of warfare, and the gender-specific division of labor on civilian and military labor markets. They stabilize these conditions or increase the dynamism of change. They have material effects because they retroact upon, and thereby shape, structural and institutional change.

These feedback relations between structure and culture/ideology are largely realized by the activities of, and conflicts between, different groups of social actors. Military modernization and gender integration are conflictual processes that affect interests of different groups inside and outside the military differently, strengthening some, while weakening others. Debates on these issues are therefore shaped by competing groups of actors fighting over status and power and employing gender ideologies to support their positions. By doing so, they influence the direction and speed of change.

Military gender integration in the US

From its outset, women's integration into the US Armed Forces has been a highly selective process largely determined by personnel demands and workforce supply. The underlying social and military tranformations are the proliferation of technology in production processes and warfare as well as the subsequent changing patterns of gender-specific division of labor in civilian and military sectors. Due to specialization and professionalization processes, military and civilian occupations have converged. This has changed recruitment conditions and led to competition between civilian and military employers for qualified personnel. Selective integration of women became necessary in the face of recruitment shortages. The establishment of the All-Volunteer Force (AVF) in 1973 has increased the dependency of the military on the female workforce, while women have also become more qualified for military jobs due to their integration in civilian labor markets. Because of discrimination against women in the civilian sector, female personnel are cheaper and on average better qualified. They represent the type of workforce that is increasingly needed in the military's growing support structure, which has to fill more jobs at lower and middle ranks with higher qualified personnel than it can attract qualified men.

These shifts in the division of labor have influenced gender ideologies concerning war and the military. The dualism of "war-prone men" and "peaceful women" remains central to constructions of military femininity and masculinity, although gender ideologies have become more diverse. They now feature images of professional female soldiers or patriotic heroines alongside more traditional depictions of women as victims in need of protection or as natural caretakers. Structural modernization has promoted gender integration, weakened the power of traditional military elites, and triggered power struggles between different military branches. Their different interests in modernization processes have contributed to the differentiation of gender ideologies.

Another important context for ideological changes is the transforming relationship between the state and the military. The dynamics between state formation and establishment of military institutions have led to a state monopoly on warfare and the "masculinization" of war. This historically grown link between state, war, and masculinity was particularly strong in nineteenth-century Europe, with its exclusively male conscript armies. At this point, ideals of military masculinity were integrated into nation-state concepts and became the basis for political participation rights. The US remained a less centralized state throughout its history; its formation was less dependent on military consolidation. The mass integration of men into a nation-state army only set in with its rise to global power. The anti-statist tradition of the US has influenced the course of military gender integration and rendered women's exclusion less rigid. Anti-statism has, however, also furthered neo-liberalization and the subsequent economization and privatization of military tasks beginning in the 1990s—developments which tend to "remasculinize" warfare. These ambivalent tendencies also influence the perception of military women.

Military gender ideologies in media representations

While the structural and institutional dimensions of gender integration have been well researched, a systematic study on the transformations of military gender ideology is so far missing. Ideological changes can be investigated by examining a public space—namely the media—in which military gender issues have been debated with some regularity and intensity throughout the past decades. Media debates provide a meta-discourse that accommodates different groups of actors. Women's integration into the US military is analyzed based on *The New York Times'* and *The Washington Post*'s reporting on military gender issues from 1990 to 2005. This theory-based, exemplary, synchronically and diachronically comparative analysis follows the methodological assumptions of Cultural Studies and Media Studies approaches (Garnham 1983; Kellner 1995; Dörner 1997), which relate media content to the social structures and relations in which they are produced. The media's embeddedness within society is expressed in its contents. It is a central arena in which values, norms, and ideologies are established and negotiated according to social power relations and conflicts of interests between different social groups. The social conditions for changing military gender ideologies can be identified by relating the analysis of social and military structures and institutions to the analysis of textual content. Critical Historical Discourse Analysis (Wodak 2001) serves as a tool for text analysis that emphasizes interrelations between text and context. It also provides a general framework for examining media content and argumentative strategies of different groups of actors.

The sample for the media analysis consists of articles dealing with women's integration into the military. By examining representations of military *women*, "gender" should not be equated with "women." Rather, images of military women are analyzed as an example for the manifestations of gender ideologies. While various studies have already focused on military masculinity, little is known about the concrete effects of changes in military structures on public representations of military femininity. Ninety-six articles (45 in *The New York Times*, 51 in *The Washington Post*) were identified by searching the newspapers' archives for the terms "women in the military," "military women," "female soldiers," and "women warriors." Their representations in the media were analyzed quantitatively and qualitatively and interpreted in relation to the structural factors influencing gender-specific division of labor in the military and beyond. For this purpose, the following categories of statements were identified from the material and their relative proportion compared across different phases of the examined time period:

- Positive statements on military women (e.g. they are courageous, patriotic, professional, reliable comrades, responsible military leaders).
- Positive statements on military gender integration (e.g. it is efficient, progressive, democratic).
- Negative statements on military women (e.g. they are physically and/or mentally unstable, natural caretakers, unfeminine).
- Negative statements on military gender integration (e.g. it is inefficient, "un-American," contradicts Western values).

The empirical analysis captures the role of different actors (military, politicians, civil society) in establishing dominant gender ideologies in media representations. It examines the conditions for the formation and change of group interests and for the success or failure of different ideological strategies. While this approach cannot grasp the position of each actor as a whole, it reliably mirrors their representation in and influence on media discourses.

War and gender as an interdisciplinary research field

During the last decades, issues of war and gender have been scrutinized in various disciplines, making the research field highly interdisciplinary. Based on the premise that war and the involved actors and institutions are parts of social systems, the relations between war and gender in different historical and cultural contexts have been thoroughly examined. This study therefore builds upon a multitude of theoretical and empirical findings.

Within the field of history, the examination of relations between war and gender was promoted by a turn towards a social history of war and by the increased inclusion of men and masculinity into accounts of gender history (Hämmerle 2000). Social history approaches do not focus on military strategy, "great men," or events such as important battles, but on the social context of warfare. They reject classical military history's idealization of traditional images of masculinity and constructions of nineteenth-century confrontations between exclusively male nation-state armies as the historical norm of war. These notions have helped make the role of women in warfare a "blind spot in cultural memory"[1] (Seifert 1996: 180). Social historians have therefore put forward case studies of women's participation in war throughout history (Frevert 1996; Hagemann and Pröve 1998; DeGroot and Peniston-Bird 2000). Their findings provide an important base for the social science study of the issue because they highlight historical changes in the gender-specific division of labor in warfare and their influence on ideology formation.

Social and cultural anthropologists have also contextualized war and military institutions within broader social developments and analyzed violent conflict as a social function determined by socio-economic conditions (Harris 1984; Carneiro 1994). Anthropological research has shown that changes in society and in warfare are deeply intertwined and that participation of women varies according to historical and cultural contexts. The forms and degree of their integration influences cultural notions on the "natural" division of labor in the case of war (Ferguson 1984). In contrast to historical sciences, this branch of anthropology aims at generalized theories. Its approaches have, however, hardly been employed in the study of modern societies, Western military institutions, or the military integration of women in the twentieth and twenty-first century.

In political science, the debate on "new wars" (Kaldor 1999; Gilbert 2003; Ruf 2003; Münkler 2005; Duffield 2005) also emphasizes the embeddedness of war within social relations. The main research interests are the contemporary changes in warfare in connection with processes such as state-failure, privatization, globalization, and neo-liberalization. The decreasing importance of nation-states opposite para- and non-state actors is discussed in relation to the phenomenon of "failed states" (Rotberg 2002; Ghani and Lockhart 2009; Starr 2011). Social science's interest in "new wars" was, however, very often stimulated from "outside," which influenced the focal points of research:

> The study of war is influenced by developments outside of science. The "attention trap" leads to high rewards for publications that deal with issues of

interest for political debates. ... The "relevance" of a particular case or issue is often ... a function of its proximity to political discussions.

(Schlichte 2002: 114)

The terrorist attacks of 9/11 and their processing in the media and in politics have particularly influenced political science research on new forms of violent conflict. In this context debates were often characterized by oversimplifications, exaggerations, and overstating of superficial similarities between disparate phenomena. The codes of the East/West conflict were replaced by the binary opposition between "old" and "new wars." Notions of political order were at times merged with theoretical positions (Schlichte 2004: 2), rendering them useful for "different institutional rhetorics and discourses of legitimation" (ibid.: 9) and providing justifications for nation- and state-building projects in Africa, Afghanistan, Iraq, or the Balkans.

The debate on "new wars" also cannot be disconnected from debates on the "crisis of the state." The enforcement and proliferation of bourgeois-capitalist structures in economy and society have caused different kinds of crises around the world. The rise in violent conflict on the sub-state level during the 1980s and 1990s, the end of the Cold War, and subsequent changes in security policy have created a "high demand for information and orientation" (ibid.: 1). In this context, the rhetoric of threat promoted by academic, military, and political security experts was widely embraced, because it blended "organized crime" and "global terrorism" and contrasted "legitimate violence" of state actors with "barbarian violence" of terrorist gangs (ibid.: 4).

Despite these biases, the debate on the "new-ness" of war has drawn political science's attention to war as a social phenomenon. This perspective has led to necessary critique of the often state-centered and ahistorical discipline of International Relations (IR). The realization that the world has not been entirely "nationalized," as often assumed during the Cold War, opened up new or marginalized perspectives on war and political violence. The debate on "new wars" also represented an opportunity to reevaluate the importance of social theory for the theory of war:

> War as a social and political phenomenon takes on too great a variety to lend itself to inductive theory development. Because each war needs to be historically contextualized, theory formation needs to build upon a historically informed theory of society. ... Only then can we focus on what is happening around the actual events of war and how these social contexts influence the manifestations of political violence.
>
> (Schlichte 2004: 11f)

The gender dimensions of new forms of conflict as well as the gender biases in theory development on these issues have so far largely been neglected (Kreisky 2008). Changes of gender relations in military institutions have also been hardly studied in relation to the transformations of warfare and political violence. At the same time, theorists like Martin Van Creveld (2000) have interpreted military gender integration as a symptom of the "feminization" of war, as Kimberly Hutchings shows in her analysis of contemporary theories on war:

> On the one hand, *feminization* refers to the fact that there are now many more women in the professional militaries of advanced industrial societies; on the other hand, *feminization* refers to a process of decline in the capacity to engage in so-called real war. ... These two meanings of *feminization* are mutually reinforcing, with each being symptom or cause of the other.
>
> (Hutchings 2008: 395)

In his concept of "humane warfare," Christopher Coker (2001, 2002) also expresses a certain nostalgia for existentialist masculinist elements in Western warfare that are allegedly still held high in other cultures (Hutchings 2008: 399). This also holds true for Herfried Münkler's (2006) concept of "postheroic war."

Besides these questionable attempts to describe the changes in warfare as "demasculinization," issues of war and gender have also been examined by feminist critics within International Relations (IR), peace and conflict research, and political science (Enloe 1990; Tickner 1992; Zalewski and Parpart 1998; Sjoberg 2010). Their approaches highlight how men and women are affected differently by war and conflict, criticize the exclusion of "interests, ideas, and experiences of women" in conflict management (Reimann 2000: 1), and deconstruct the (de-)gendering of theory and empirical research in IR. A feminist redefinition of security that includes environmental and social security is often part of the research program viewing the military as antithetical to these objectives (Tickner 2001: 62). International strategies for conflict resolution are evaluated for their potential to reproduce power relations and gender inequality (ibid.: 8f.). These approaches are closely connected to the peace movement but have an ambivalent relationship to images of women as morally superior and peaceful (Peach 1996: 178ff.), images that have been deconstructed as essentially military ideologies (Enloe 1988: 72).

Military sociologists have also argued that military institutions need to be analyzed as interacting with social processes. In European research, (de-)constructivist approaches (Seifert 1995; Eifler and Seifert 1999) have dominated since the 1990s. The focus has mainly been on the "symbolic function of the military for gender constructions" (Gabbert 2007: 11). These studies inquire "how discrimination can be reduced and how "hegemonic masculinity" in the military is changing" (ibid.: 12). The construction of the fighter as an exclusively male figure (Seifert 1996), and mechanisms supporting military masculinity, are major research issues in micro-sociological, inner-military analyses examining the perspective of the involved individuals. Because integration is often conceptualized as a "reaction to demands for gender equality" (ibid.: 14), the complex reciprocity between social and military developments and the different push and pull factors relevant to the military integration of women are often understudied. Within US debates, Jean Bethke Elshtain's *Women and War* (1987) is considered an essential standard work that elucidates the relations between gender constructions and symbolic representations of war and peace in an explorative study of symbols, myths, and discourses of gender and collective violence. Elshtain identifies the opposition of "Just Warrior and Beautiful Soul" as a dominant image constantly reproduced to the present day. In a similar vein, Joshua Goldstein (2001) outlines how gender is embedded into cultural conceptions of war and aggression.

Other important contributions that deal with the relation between the military and gender ideology include Susan Jeffords' (1989) analysis of popular culture representations of military masculinity after Vietnam. The work of Nira Yuval-Davis (1997) treats the relations between gender, military, and nationalism. Cynthia Enloe (2000) has examined the process of militarization and its negative impact on women's lives and status in society. Melissa S. Herbert (2000) has revealed how servicewomen create and recreate their identities as a woman soldier, and how they experience and deal with the military's masculine ideology. Carol Burke (2004) has investigated military basic training and the role of gender ideology in accomplishing military conformity and discipline. She argues that the gendering of initiation rites marginalizes female recruits and promotes sexual aggression against them. Seifert (1995) divides the US research field according to political standpoints into "peace ethicists" (e.g. Ruddick 1982) who oppose women's military integration based on pacifist motives, and "equality ethicists" (e.g. Stiehm 1989; Holm 1982) supporting women's right to equal participation.

US military sociologists (Segal 1995; Booth *et al.* 2000) have considered structural changes affecting women's participation in great depth and have highlighted the social and military conditions under which integration is furthered or hindered. The analysis of structural aspects of integration processes in the present study is largely based on their evidence. In Segal's often-cited model (Segal 1995) and its adaptations (Iskra *et al.* 2002), cultural aspects are listed among political, economic, and strategic factors and are considered less influential than the others. The relationship between these different dimensions so far remained understudied. Helena Carreiras (2006) has developed a theoretical framework for analyzing the interactions between economic, cultural, political, and military factors that influence different military gender integration patterns. Her multidimensional analysis focuses on different levels, from the macro-societal to the interpersonal. The influence of gender-specific labor division and orga-nizational change in the military are also discussed as important variables. The role of culture/ideology, however, remains under-theorized and is at times equated with the "individual/subjective" level.

All in all, many theoretical concepts and empirical data on the structural and cultural dimensions of integration processes are available as foundations for studying military gender ideology. The challenge lies in conceptualizing and systematically analyzing the relationship between these different dimensions. The reward is a better understanding of the nexus between military restructuring processes, the gender-specific division of military labor, and changes of gender ideologies.

2 Relations between the material and the cultural

The interactions between military transformations, labor market developments, and gender ideology require clarifying how the relationship between socio-economic relations, social structures, and military institutions on the one hand, and cultural constructions and ideology on the other is best conceptualized. This approach should reveal the specific interactions between structural and ideological change. The relationship between the material and the cultural is, of course, one of the main issues of social science theory and research and also one of its main "battlefields." A wide and often confusing array of approaches has been developed to grasp this issue. According to the historical and political contexts of their development, different schools of thought have put forward different explanatory models and have evaluated the relative importance of each side of the equation. The possibility of a distinct analytical separation between different levels of social reality has become increasingly doubtful. These historical traditions need to be considered in formulating an approach tailored to the research interest at hand. They provide the basis for an undogmatic "theory mix" that relates to the specific research questions and to the analyzed material, enables both text and context analysis, and introduces a dynamic model to conceptualize their interrelatedness. The merits of this theoretical endeavor can then be evaluated through confrontation with the empirical material.

Materialism as a research strategy

Grounding ideological phenomena within the socio-economic relations of their production has been a major concern of materialist theory since the writings of Marx and Engels. Countless critiques and further developments of materialist thinking have been put forward to this day. Nonetheless, even though—or perhaps because—so much effort has been made to refute, defend, or adapt materialism, the concept has become relatively blurred and charged with preconceptions. Any researcher today announcing to work on a specific social phenomenon by employing a materialist approach is bound to be misunderstood. Some may even argue that the term is best avoided when clarifying theoretical perspectives. Materialism is often equated with "Marxism," "historical materialism," "realism," "positivism," "economism," or "determinism," all of which tend to inspire polemic rejection. Even though materialist approaches are burdened with a complex history of ideas and often met with prejudice they can help focus our attention on socio-economic relations, patterns of labor division, and their interaction with cultural and ideological conceptions. They not only emphasize the importance of socio-economic structures and institutions theoretically, but provide a research strategy to actually study them.

The history of materialist concepts in philosophical and social science traditions cannot and need not be detailed here. Nonetheless, important cornerposts of a working definition of materialism need to be identified by briefly examining the relevant forms of use and associated controversies. The focal point of this endeavor is social and political science research practice and the concrete research questions and objectives of the study. We seek an undogmatic definition of materialism, one that is not derived from the *issue* of the analysis, but from its explanatory model and argumentation structure. This keeps "classic" constructivist or post-structuralist topics such as gender, discourse, identity, or media within reach. A productive combination of different approaches that deal with the relation between material and cultural phenomena, between social relations and ideology, is essential.

Marx's work remains the starting point for social science engagement with materialist theory. His oeuvre is extensive and can be read with different motivations and interests. It is open to debate which aspects of Marx' theoretical thinking are crucial for understanding his social theory—clarifying these questions is the task of the numerous historians of ideas who have and continue to compete for superior insights into Marx's writings. What can be said with some degree of certainty is, however, that in *German Ideology* (Marx 1962) and *Theses on Feuerbach* (Marx 1998), Marx turned his attention towards "human practice" and human nature as a product of "social relations" and the "material conditions of production." He assumed that the historically specific mode of production was decisive for understanding the dynamics of social change and conceptualized a relationship of dependence between different levels of social reality (economic, juristic/political, ideological) with causal priority on the "economic base." It is disputed whether Marx's theorizing is applicable to any other phenomenon than his own research object: the capitalist state in nineteenth-century Europe. This is, of course, a question of abstraction. Marx's theories on the transformation from feudalism to capitalism relate to a historically and spatially specific phenomenon. An ahistorical theory of development or a stage model for all cultural development is not incorporated within them (Heinrich 1999: 151). They do, however, include a great deal of generalization and can therefore be viewed as a research program to examine differences and similarities within and between social systems (Harris 2001: 229).

The critiques and further developments of Marx's and Engels' approaches are as versatile as the original opus itself. Beginning in the 1920s, a new tradition, often summarized as "Western Marxism" (Jay 1984) or neo-Marxism, has emerged from this. Its representatives—George Lukács, Louis Althusser, Antonio Gramsci, or Theodor Adorno—conceptualized a "humanist, subjectivist and undogmatic Marxism that was the negation of its official Soviet (or Eastern) counterparts" (ibid.: 2) and challenged the scientific self-consciousness of Marxism. Different non-Marxist influences, such as psycho-analysis, existentialism, and structuralism, were integrated into Western Marxist theories.

Even beyond Western Marxism, a "distinct generation of non-dogmatically leftist intellectuals" (Jay 1984: 19) can be identified that builds upon Marx's theses: Nicos Poulantzas (1978) developed his critique of the state building upon Althusser (1977); Moishe Postone (1996) refers to Adorno (1974) and the Frankfurt School in his analyses of the transformations of capitalism; Ernesto Laclau and Chantal Mouffe (1987) follow Gramsci's concept of hegemony (1999) in their project of post-Marxism. Recent decades have also seen renewed interest in economy-critical studies, among them Elmar Altvater's analysis of globalization processes, which builds on Marx's theory on money and crises (Altvater 2006). Cultural Studies have also been influenced by Western Marxism and build upon Adorno's and Horkheimer's critique of cultural industry (1947). Raymond Williams' concept of Cultural Materialism (Williams 1980) and Douglas Kellner's work on "media culture" (1995) stand in this tradition. Foucault's theory of power (1980) and Bourdieu's theory of capital (1986), as well as feminist and post-colonial approaches, have also been developed in interaction with Marxism and have enriched materialist approaches through their interventions. Important criticism has been formulated to improve the applicability and adaptability of materialist social theory for current research.

A frequent problem facing materialist theory is a tendency towards economistic, mono-causal reductionism that deduces all social phenomena from economic relations and thereby conceptualizes political and ideological superstructures as dependent, reacting entities. Representatives of the Western Marxist tradition have tended to focus on this problem. Lukács (1923) has striven to revaluate the category of consciousness within Marx's theory, and Gramsci (1999) has developed his concept of hegemony to grasp the importance of the ideological level for social change. Althusser (1977) has focused on the reproduction of the conditions of production within ideological state apparatuses, which mediate concepts of morality, citizen consciousness, and professional ethos. According to Althusser, ideology plays a crucial role in this reproduction process and is thus always already incorporated within the conditions of production. This concept includes a theory of the state in which the state is not limited to its repressive and regulatory functions but includes ideological reproduction as well. The school system was Althusser's case study for an ideological state apparatus, but he also emphasized the military's double role as a means of repressive and ideological control in the name of state power.

This vein of ideology critique has reconsidered Marx's and Engels' views on ideology as "false consciousness" that deceives individuals about the reality they live in, paralyzes their political power, and thereby supports the ruling class. Althusser aimed at identifying the interests behind ideology production and ideology's function as a strategy for maintaining power. At the same time, he renounced the notion of ideology as a form of consciousness and reconceptualized it as a form of meaningful practice that constitutes the subjects and has a material component as well. Accordingly, ideology is found not only within the mind, but also within institutions. Building upon Althusser, Stuart Hall defined ideology as "mental frames" that different social groups develop to make sense of social practice. Language is the central medium in which ideology is produced and transformed (Hall 1983: 21). The degree to which a particular ideology distorts reality remains open within this conceptualization. This leads to the abandonment of the true/false dualism, while still emphasizing the grounding of ideology in material relations.

The pronounced concern of Western and neo-Marxism with consciousness, culture, and ideology has at the same time led to a neglect of economic issues:

> Culture [became] a central concern of the tradition, which tended as a result to neglect the economy and, at times, politics. Western Marxism, therefore, meant a Marxism that was far more dialectic than materialist ... . Western Marxism has enriched cultural theory more than economic or political theory.
>
> (Jay 1984: 3, 9)

An in-depth analysis of the influence of socio-economic and military structures on gender ideology therefore needs to be based on a more balanced materialist approach, one that values the role of ideology for social change and at the same time refocuses on the broader social transformations underlying structural and ideological phenomena.

In the 1960s, Marvin Harris and other US cultural and social anthropologists began to develop a materialism that sought to avoid the common traps of Marxist theory, among them economistic determinism, dialectical philosophy of history, concepts of rigid class antagonisms, and Eurocentrism, while at the same time not losing sight of the causal priority of social relations. This involved developing a dynamic conception of the relations between mode of production, form of political organization, and ideology. In the context of his discipline's belated recognition of materialist theory, Harris (1994) argued against the limitation to ethnographic methods in anthropology and against a narrow definition of culture as a solely mental phenomenon. He advocated a concept of culture as a material process as well as theory development that regards social structures, institutions, systems, and political economy as important categories of analysis.

While this cultural materialism was established to enable the analysis of "prehistoric" and/or civilizations without written records, the specific research interests of anthropology have highlighted central weaknesses of Marxist analysis, such as its Eurocentrism, progress-oriented evolutionism, and the equation of history and class struggle. In this process, cultural materialists have identified adaptable aspects of Marx' theory for social science. Harris (2001: 240) saw these aspects in: (1) the trisection of socio-cultural systems, (2) the explanation of socio-political organization and ideology as adaptations to infrastructural conditions, (3) the formulation of a functional model, in which interactive effects between all parts of the system are conceivable, and 4) the possibility to distinguish between system-maintaining and system-destroying variables. Cultural materialists assume that the material conditions of social life are the domineering influence on the development of society (Harris 1979: 141). Social structures, institutions, and socio-economic relations shape changes in ideologies, ideas, beliefs, and values more than vice versa. The cultural level is, however, not considered a mere by-product of material phenomena. As the cultural level stabilizes social systems or facilitates change through positive or negative feedback, it does have material effects:

> [This model] holds that, over time, changes in a society's material base will lead to functionally compatible changes in its social and political institutions (structure) and in its secular and religious ideology (superstructure). ... Regardless of the apparent neatness of this model, [it] does not posit a simplistic, mechanistic correspondence between material conditions (infrastructure) and structural and ideological phenomena. It never suggests that *all* changes in the system under *all* circumstances spring from alterations in the infrastructure. Nor does [it] claim that the structure and superstructure are passive entities that do not influence the material base. [It] proposes a probabilistic relationship between these three levels, while at the same time insisting that the *principal* forces of change reside in the material conditions of human existence.
>
> (Murphy and Margolis 1995: 2f.)

Harris (1994: 68) refined Marx's trisection of social systems into base, political, and ideological superstructures by introducing the concepts of infrastructure, structure, and superstructure. He defined infrastructure as the "conjunction of demographic, technological, economic, and ecological processes—the modes of production and reproduction" and as the field of interaction between social systems and their environment. Accordingly, infrastructure consists not only of a mode of production but also of a mode of reproduction. Structure is the level of social organization in which political and economic acquisition and distribution takes place (Elwell 1991: 7). Structure and superstructure (values, beliefs, norms, ideologies) influence the pace and form of change. All levels of social systems are related to each other through feedback-relations. Social transformations take on dynamics due to conflicts of interests between different socio-economic groups of actors, not due to class struggle between antagonistic blocs. This last definition helps incorporate the manifold differentiations and conflicts between groups of social actors within different social fields.

The relationship between the different levels of social formations is highly dynamic. Even Marx did not envision a mechanistic, linear causal relationship between base and superstructure. Historical materialism assumes a structural dependency of different social levels and not a determination of one event by another (Heinrich 1999: 148). The focus of interest is on the interaction between different social levels, not on '"simplistic" explanations in terms of a single factor' or an "absolute one-to-one-effect" (Harris 1979: 159). Such a conception helps analyze the functions of different characteristics of society for its development and transformation without arguing for a static structural functionalism (Harris 2001: 235). It scrutinizes the changing functionality of different ideological formations in regard to the changing socio-economic conditions. Hence, the challenge for an analysis of the relations between military and social change and gender ideologies lies in identifying the functions these ideologies have under specific socio-economic, technological, strategic, and demographic conditions.

Various cultural materialist studies have examined aspects of this issue by emphasizing the embeddedness of war and military institutions within social relations and structures. Harris (1984) has shown that form and organization of warfare depend on the technological, demographic, and economic conditions within the warring societies. Modes of warfare influence the gender-specific division of labor in the event of war, which in turn influences the respective ideologies on femininity and masculinity. By employing Max Weber's theory of bureaucratization (Weber 1922), Elwell (1991) has shown that changes in the US mode of production have entailed a highly specialized division of labor, enabling the increased efficiency that is required in the face of industrialization, advancement of technological complexity, and expanding populations. On the superstructural level these developments are expressed through a process Weber termed rationalization, which increases the importance of scientific rationalism, individualism, discipline, and calculability (Elwell 1991: 15f.). Military institutions have also been affected by these transformations which have shaped military and civilian labor markets and "rationalized" associated gender ideologies. Maxine Margolis (2000) outlines the relationship between modes of production, gender-specific division of labor, and perceptions of masculinity and femininity in US history. According to her model, social structures—in which men and women are incorporated differently according to socio-economic group or institution—determine cultural expressions of this differential positioning. Perceptions of gender roles are established in adaptation to and for the stabilization of historically varying forms of labor division. Increased labor market participation of women has revolutionized notions of accepted gender roles and behavior.

Gender Studies and feminist theory have always had an ambivalent relationship with materialist theory. The general tendency within gender research over the past decades has been to focus on subjectivity, performativity, identity, and discourse. For gender and military research, this has yielded insights into gendered practices and ideas, contributed to the understanding of masculinism and its functions within military institutions, and highlighted the process of identity formation of service members. While structural and institutional analysis also has a strong tradition within gender and military research, little has been done to relate these analyses systematically to the changes in military culture and gender ideology.

Gender theory's unease with materialism partly reflects Marx's neglect of the female workforce in his theoretical writings. The gratis housework done by women, for example, was omitted within his theories of value and commodity; the division of labor within the family was interpreted as a natural relation. Thereby, female labor was made invisible within production processes (Neusüß 1985). This Androcentrism was continuously reproduced in materialist theory through analysis and political strategy. With the rising interest in culture and ideology promoted by Western Marxism, however, a tradition of materialist feminism developed. It asked "how historical materialism might be used to explain and change women's oppression and exploitation under capitalism" (Hennessy/Ingraham 1997: 10). Its representatives pointed to the deficits of feminism and Marxism alike, and aimed at a synthesis: "Classical marxist insights into history were gender blind and ignored women's contribution to social production, while feminist analysis—although strong regarding the systemic character of relations between the sexes—was often ahistorical and insufficiently materialist" (ibid.: 6). Common ground was found in the assumption of the centrality of labor division in configurating gender relations: "The tradition of feminist engagement with marxism emphasizes a perspective on social life that refuses to separate the materiality of meaning, identity, the body, state, or nation from the prerequisite division of labor" (ibid.: 1).

Despite various differences and conflicts within materialist feminism, such as debates on the definition of the material or the relationship between patriarchy and capitalism, these approaches have distinguished themselves from tendencies within Gender Studies to exclude political economy and relations of power from the analysis of gender relations and focus on "abstract, ahistorical, or merely cultural categories like desire, matter, or performativity" (ibid.: 2). For this purpose, the material base of ideology is recognized without equating ideology and material practices. Both the concept of ideology as a direct reflection of social relations as well as the classical Marxist perception of ideology as "false consciousness" are renounced: "Ideology is embedded historically in material practice but it does not follow *either* that ideology is theoretically indistinguishable from material practice or that it bears any direct relationship to them" (Barrett 1997: 93).

Conceptualizations of gender ideologies as expressions of material conditions—mediated through social and political institutions, structures, and relations—remain a relevant topic for Gender Studies. While concepts of masculinity and femininity are based on the division of labor between men and women, the gendered practices and ideas derived from it transcend the division between the biologically defined sexes. The gendering of social phenomena (e.g. the portrayal of the nation as a woman in need of protection or the image of warfare as a male endeavor) is the consequence of the ideologically charged character of gender constructions. As the debate on intersectionality (Crenshaw 1991; Brah/Phoenix 2004; Becker-Schmidt 2008) has highlighted, gender cannot be perceived as a privileged category of analysis but has to be understood in its interaction with other forms of social inequality such as class, nationality, or ethnicity.

No systematic in-depth analysis of the relations between structural and ideological change has been put forward within the field of gender and military research. This study is therefore designed to test the hypothesis that changes in production processes and warfare—most importantly the increased complexity of technology and differentiation of work fields—have favored selective integration of women on civilian and military labor markets. These processes have transformed and diversified ideologies in regard to gender and the military and have made them a tool in conflicts of interest in the course of military modernization after the end of the Cold War. Military gender ideologies fulfill different functions for military and non-military actors, such as political elites, NGOs, lobbyists, etc., legitimizing their stance on different foreign, military, or gender policy issues. They are crucial in adapting integration patterns to the military's needs by enabling a modernized view of women's abilities and suitability for some tasks while referring to traditional notions to justify exclusions from others.

Based on different schools of materialist thinking, a research strategy to analyze the relations between social and military change and the transformations of military gender ideology can be developed. This approach gives causal priority to the material conditions of social practice in the analysis of ideological change and acknowledges the centrality of production processes, labor division, as well as technological, demographic, and economic change for the analysis of gender relations. At the same time, it does not deny the importance of political power relations, conflicts of interest, and ideology in the stabilization or change of social systems. For this purpose, ideology is not viewed as a solely mental, but as an institutional phenomenon. While gender and military research provides extensive data for establishing structural and institutional contexts and identifying contextual factors that influence gender ideology, ideological transformations have yet to be operationalized and systematically analyzed. Media representations provide a suitable body of data to exemplify these ideological changes.

Media representations as an object of social science research

Because the research interest focuses on the relation between social and political conditions and conflicts on the one side and military gender ideologies on the other, it is insufficient to study military gender issues in terms of policy outcomes. Rather, we need a unit of analysis that features public struggles over constructions of gender, war, and the military, such as media discourses. They are embedded within social relations and their contents can be studied as effects of the social conditions of their production, distribution, and consumption, upon which they also retroact. Media debates articulate conflicts of interest between different social groups. They represent a central arena in which norms, values, and ideologies are established in adaptation to social relations of power (Kellner 1995). Media content analysis therefore enables conclusions to be drawn on changes in the ideological realm. The operationalization of these theoretical assumptions requires media analysis that is well-grounded in social theory:

> [M]edia cultural texts are neither merely vehicles of a dominant ideology, nor pure and innocent entertainment. Rather they are complex artifacts that

embody social and political discourses whose analysis and interpretation require methods of reading and critique that articulate their embeddedness in the political economy, social relations, and the political environment within which they are produced, circulated, and received.

(Kellner 1995: 4)

Materialist media theory has investigated the media's embeddedness within social structures in the context of Marxist social theory. The main research interests were the analysis of media (companies) within the capitalist system, their function in stabilizing class relations and in the reproduction of the work-force, and the imbalance of power between production and reception. In Western Europe, Media Studies have mostly developed within cultural studies and have concentrated on text analysis rather than empirical social analysis (Garnham 1983). This has established a linguistic, discourse-oriented, and/or psychoanalytical mainstream. At the same time, the US tradition was dominated by functionalist approaches that focused on the effects of media consumption ("impact studies") (ibid.: 316ff.). These developments hindered the formulation of a comprehensive social science approach and called for a re-establishment of Media Studies' links with "the mainland of social science" (ibid.: 314).

Cultural Studies[2] gave new impulses to Media Studies in this regard during the 1980s and 1990s. They inspired renewed interest in power and dominance by referring to the media critique of Adorno and Horkheimer (1947) (Kleiner 2006: 269), who had pointed out the role of mass media for the reproduction of capitalist economy and its social system. Building upon their approach, Cultural Studies have based their research on a concept of culture that did not differentiate between "high" and "popular culture." Both were studied as fields of social power struggles. The media have been an important field of research since the 1960s, for they are seen as a central means by which the ideologies of the dominant social groups are inscribed into society. Ideology is not considered a message, but a text which incorporates material and cultural elements. In their research on the media, Cultural Studies have focused on ethnographic analysis and media reception in everyday contexts and different subcultures. On the methodological level, they combined participative observation and interviews with text analysis (Hepp/ Winter 2003) and thereby moved Media Studies in the direction of social analysis. Raymond Williams (1980) took up this challenge by putting forward his concept of Cultural Materialism.[3] He welcomed research on reception, but criticized audience studies for neglecting economic, sociocultural, and technological factors. Social contexts and economic interests that shape the structures of the media were emphasized as important aspects of media analysis.

Douglas Kellner's critique of Cultural Studies research practice (1995) has articulated a similar claim. Kellner has advocated more strongly embedding media content analysis within social theory: "[C]ultural studies cannot be done without social theory, ... we need to understand the structures and dynamics of a given society to understand and interpret its culture" (Kellner 1995: 4). His concept of "media culture" refers to Adorno's media critique, but speaks out against the conception of a passive audience. From a media pedagogy point of view, he pointed out the emancipatory potential of popular culture and searched for a compromise between the political-economic macro-approaches of Marxist analysis and the "populist" approaches that celebrated the audience's freedom and creativity in decoding media texts (Dörner 1997: 320). Kellner criticized the over-emphasis on text and reception analysis and the neglect of conditions of production as well as the political economy of texts (Kellner 1995: 41). He argued for systematically incorporating both the material foundations of cultural products and the surrounding socio-political debates and conflicts into the interpretation and analysis of texts.

Kellner's critique helped establish a foundation for social and political science analysis of media content that aims at relating cultural products to social and political relations of power. His model of contextualization is, however, limited to relating texts to other contemporary texts and discourses (Dörner 1997: 327). From a political science point of view, the process of contextualizing has to include social science know-how and debates beyond Cultural Studies which have tended to draw a rather simplified image of the political process, the functions of the public, and the ideological lines of conflict within contemporary society (ibid.). Building upon Kellner's understanding of Cultural Studies and social and political science interventions, media gender ideologies regarding war and the military can be analyzed in relation to the gender-specific structuring of labor markets and military institutions. Findings on social and military transformations and political relations of power provide the groundwork for interpreting media content. Media production and consumption, media companies and their audiences are part of the same social system. Accordingly, text analysis alone is insufficient to grasp and explain sociopolitical transformations and conflicts. Text and context represent equally important levels of analysis.

The media, the military, and political elites in the US

Since the Second World War, during which the military and the government were protected against independent media reporting by a system of censorship, the relationship between media and military has been tense. Military representatives often perceived the media as an operational and career risk, but were at the same time dependent on them in their pursuit of public support. After the Vietnam War, tension was added by the belief that military defeat had been a result of critical coverage and uncensored access of reporters to the theater of war. A survey of the *Freedom Forum First Amendment Center* found in 1995 that 64 percent of officers still believed that media reporting had exerted a negative impact on the war effort in Vietnam. Almost all surveyed officers expressed antipathy towards journalists (Belknap 2001: 1ff.). Media representatives also regularly range behind military leaders in terms of the public's trust and respect in surveys (Dunsmore 1996: 16).

Embedding of media content within social relations raises questions on the relationship between the media and political elites. The Vietnam War and the UN intervention in Somalia in 1992/93 have often been cited as examples for the media's power over the government's foreign policy decisions. Empirical analyses of war reporting have, however, refuted the thesis of an "oppositional media," which assumes that the media develop their own stance on policy issues and can enforce it on the political elite. Daniel Hallin has shown that the media mostly support political elites uncritically, as long as those elites are unified on a particular issue. As soon as conflicts arise, media reporting becomes more ambivalent and can even change sides completely when one group gains power over the other:

> Neither the institutional structure nor the professional ideology of the media had changed substantially [during the war in Vietnam], but in a changed political environment these could have very different implications for the reporting of the news. ... In short, then, the case of Vietnam suggests that whether the media tend to be supporting or critical of government policies depends on the degree of consensus those policies enjoy, particularly within the political establishment.
>
> (Hallin 1984: 22)

Analyses of the reporting on the Somalia intervention (Robinson 2001) have also shown that no "CNN effect" exists that can force the political and military leadership to deploy the Armed Forces in an area of crisis. Only when the US government had already been preparing the military intervention in Somalia, the media started broadcasting the suffering of the Somali people to legitimize US involvement. The withdrawal from Somalia was also not caused by media images of killed US soldiers, but by how these images were interpreted in the context of power struggles between civilian and military leadership. If a change in media representations can be observed, the explanation lies in the changing social, political, and military conditions of reporting. These determine whether the media support or criticize a certain political course.

An important context for the relationship of the media to political and military elites is also the structural development of the media market. During the period investigated here, the US media market experienced a trend towards monopolization and commercialization, which affected the forms and contents of reporting. Compared to European media, US media have always been more commercialized. They are financially more dependent on advertising and more often traded on the stock market (Benson and Hallin 2007). The revolution of digital technology has strengthened these tendencies because the introduction of digital transmission was affordable only for large companies (Prokop 2001: 409). This not only affected audiovisual media, but print publications as well. Reduced state regulation promoted a wave of fusions that brought many print media companies under the ownership of large media conglomerates (ibid.: 416). Newspapers were in many cases bought up, rationalized, and reoriented towards sensationalist reporting (ibid.: 394).

Reporting on military issues after the Vietnam War has been shaped by the conditions of an increasingly competitive news market. This has promoted uncritical reporting and propagandistic depictions of war. The economic weakening of many media companies has led to a greater dependency on military decision-makers (Franklin 1994: 40ff.). Technological advances in communication and warfare have at the same time facilitated manipulation of and through the media. The successful media image of the Persian Gulf War in 1991 as a just, clean, and overwhelmingly victorious "Techno War" is a case in point. The military and government controlled the distribution of information, while mass media generated support for government policies (Jeffords/Rabinovitz 1994: 2ff.). Only large media networks gained access (albeit limited and controlled) to the theatre of war. Only reporters from those newspapers and TV networks that had supported the intervention in advance were allowed into the media pools.

The practice of "embedded" reporting has further promoted journalists' dependency on and identification with the military's point of view. Operation Iraqi Freedom featured a high degree of fictionalized propaganda, such as the staged toppling of the statue of Saddam Hussein or the rescue of POW Jessica Lynch. The "media disaster" of the Somalia intervention shows, however, that the government's control over war reporting can be lost when political restructuring takes place or when conflicts of interests arise between different parts of the military and political elite. The torture scandal in Abu Ghraib prison also openly questioned the government's control over that war and its public representation. Now, soldiers can easily send emails and digital photographs home: these records influence media images of the war as well. If and how these images and texts are received and discussed, however, depends less on the technological possibilities than on the social and political contexts within which they are produced and interpreted. Neither the government, nor the military or the media can be perceived as an overwhelmingly powerful manipulative force. The instable and contested power relations between them are decisive.

Critical Historical Discourse Analysis as a tool for text analysis

Refined concepts of ideology and its relation to material conditions from different materialist perspectives provide a general theoretical framework to analyze the interaction between structural and ideological military change. Materialist feminism and Gender Studies point to the importance of gender-specific division of labor for the construction of gender ideologies. Media and Cultural Studies explain the role of the media in ideology production. They also show how the social embeddedness of media texts can be conceptualized. Since newspaper articles represent the primary research material, we still need a more concrete procedure for text analysis, one that enables textual contents to be related to social structures, institutions, and conflicts.

Critical Historical Discourse Analysis (CHDA) (Wodak 2001) provides such a framework for context-oriented text analysis. The notion of discourse has been widely debated as a theoretical concept in social science for the last decades. Mostly, it is associated with post-structuralist perspectives on how social reality is permeated by the interrelations between knowledge and power. Discourse is considered a system of meaning that constitutes social reality and produces notions of truth. Developed within linguistics, CHDA features a "particular interest in the relation between language and power" (ibid.: 2) and regards language as a form of social and political action. Far from being bound to post-structuralist premises, it is open to different conceptions of the relation between the material and the ideological, different research interests, and different definitions of context and can therefore be used as a framework for interpreting text in relation to the social conditions of its production. It emphasizes contextualization of discourse within historical, social, and political transformations and thereby helps formulate social science research interests for textual analysis. In the first step, CHDA identifies the main contents of a particular discourse which are extracted from the research material. In the second step, argumentative strategies employed by different groups of actors and wider sociopolitical contests of discourses are established.

Media discourses have been an important arena for debates on military gender issues in the US during the past decades. Debates on women's integration into the US Armed Forces have been particularly heated and therefore represent an ideal case study to exemplify transformations in military gender ideologies. The influential and prestigious US daily newspapers *The New York Times* (*NYT*)[4] and *The Washington Post* (*WP*)[5] lend themselves well to the analysis of broadly recognized debates on important policy issues. They enable observation of changes in the positions of military, political, and intellectual elites because these media outlets are widely perceived as "opinion leaders" on the news market. The specific *contents* of reporting must be considered in the context of the position of these papers within the liberal mainstream. They by no means represent all social groups. Content *changes* are nevertheless informative about the influence of changing structural conditions on gender ideologies and indicate continuities and turning points of discourses.

By searching the newspapers' archives for the search terms "women in the military," "military women," "female soldiers," and "women warriors," 96 newspaper articles (45 from *The New York Times*, 51 from *The Washington Post*; including 40 reports[6], 23 features[7], and 33 editorials[8])[9] were identified that dealt with military gender integration from 1990 to 2005. News summaries, wire copies, letters to the editor, or descriptive accounts, e.g. on committee ballot results or on court proceedings in cases of sexual harassment, were excluded from the sample. Articles that did not refer to current integration issues, for example reporting on a memorial for women Vietnam veterans, were also excluded.[10]

In the analysis of these media discourses, the article contents were situated within military as well as within broader social and political contexts. These various contexts were established by the findings of political science, International

Relations, and gender and military research. The text analyses were related to those contextual factors that influence gender-specific division of labor and thereby the quantity and quality in women's military integration. The participation of different groups of actors in media debates was investigated. The relevant actors include the military, the civilian leadership, civil society agents and organizations, such as lobbyists and NGOs, as well as the journalists as the authors of the analyzed articles. Statements from "outside" represent a particularly important interface between reporting and social contexts: they reflect the structural positioning of different groups of actors and their conclusive interests in military transformation processes. Comparing different phases of the investigated period helps identify effects of changing conditions on gender ideologies and the functions they attained for different actors.

The 1990 to 2005 investigation period was selected to include different phases of military labor market development: general downsizing of personnel and changes in its qualitative make-up in the face of technological and strategic modernization after the end of the Cold War versus increased recruitment efforts for various military interventions as well as different political power relations within the civilian leadership and between civilian and military realms. The early 1990s mark the beginning of rising female representation in the Armed Forces and the lifting of many exclusionary policies. The final year, 2005, marks the official end of major combat operations in Iraq. This time frame was divided into three periods according to central turning points in integration processes:

- Phase 1 from 1990 to 1994 includes the intervention in the Persian Gulf in 1991, the first large-scale military intervention since the establishment of the All-Volunteer-Force (AVF). It coincides with comprehensive measures to integrate women, such as lifting bans on their deployment on combat ships and aircrafts or the rescinding of the so-called "risk-rule" that banned women from ground combat support troops.
- Phase 2 from 1995 to 1999 represents a period in which many of these measures were implemented and women's participation rose, while personnel were downsized and no larger military interventions took place.
- Phase 3 from 2000 to 2005 experienced the expansionist military policies and major military interventions of the "War on Terror," which was accompanied by neoconservative, antifeminist hegemony in civilian politics.

In addition to analyzing general debates on gender integration, several case studies on war reporting were scrutinized for the employment of gender stereotypes. These highlight how coverage of particular events relates to the general tendencies in media debates on military women. For the early 1990s, the analysis focuses on the UN intervention in Somalia 1992/93, especially the capture and killing of US soldiers in Mogadishu in October 1993. This intervention and its tragic failure were often depicted as a "demasculinization" of the Armed Forces and the USA in general. No gender-sensitive analysis of these media interpretations has yet been advanced, as opposed to the Persian Gulf War in 1991, which inspired in-depth critiques of gendered representations. For the "War on Terror," reporting on the capture of US soldier Jessica Lynch by Iraqi forces in 2003 and the involvement of Private Lynndie England in the torture scandal of Abu Ghraib in 2004 were selected as case studies. Reporting on both events was highly gendered and implicitly or explicitly related to the issue of gender in the military in media discourses.

3 Gender, state, and the military

State formation, militarization, and women's exclusion: historical interrelations

If military, social, and political conditions help determine gender ideology, then these conditions need to be specified to make sense of ideological change. This task raises the question of the general relationship between social, political, and military organization and gender-specific inclusions and exclusions. Since the military represents a social sub-system, it cannot be analyzed as an isolated entity. We need to look at broader social developments, as well as historical preconditions, to understand why gender-specific labor division has changed inside and outside the military. The relations between socio-economic production, state transformation, and modes of warfare provide the main context for the establishment and evolution of military gender ideologies.

The nineteenth century is a suitable starting point for examining the relationship between modern military institutions and gender ideology. Within this time frame, the nation-state was established as the dominant model of socio-political organization across Europe and with it the nation-state military as the institutional basis for modern warfare. During the same period, dichotomized gender images of women as emotional, passive, and peaceful versus men as rational, active, and war-prone were established. Following the propositions of ideology critique, these gender ideologies must be related to the socio-economic and political conditions under which they were produced. The emergence of the modern nation-state and of the military as the central state institution legitimized to execute violence were important contexts for the development of the nexus between war and dualistic gender constructions. Grasping this relationship requires acknowledging that the state's monopoly on warfare is a historically specific phenomenon. Nationalization and militarization of warfare in Europe began in the sixteenth century and were consolidated with the establishment of sovereign nation-states. This development has been at the root of the successive exclusion of women from warfare.

In Europe, the historical dependency of state formation on acquiring and protecting territorial gains initiated a dynamic relationship between state-building and military structures: the military enabled the centralization and sovereignty of the emerging nation-states, the centralized states helped consolidate the military through financial support (taxes) and human resources (conscription). Territorial warfare under the social, technological, and economic conditions of the nineteenth and early twentieth century depended on state control over broad masses of men and their integration into military apparatuses. Warfare was thus "masculinized." Since state-building processes were based on military consolidation, this masculinization also affected ideas of citizenship. The result was the idealization of war-prone masculinity and the integration of this ideal into the notion of the modern citizen. The state and the military were both defined as male resources of power based on structures of male-bonding (Kreisky 1992).

Women's exclusion is a result of this historically grown institutionalization of military masculinity. It is grounded in the development of modern political organization and in the transformation of mercenary to nation-state armies. The European armies of early modern times had no concept of gender-based exclusion from warfare. They functioned like mobile villages and depended on female labor. In wars between local rulers, women had a vital position in supply and logistics and moved with the fighting mercenaries. No strict separation of military and civilian life existed (Hacker 1981). These conditions began to erode with the invention of fire arms at the turn from the sixteenth to the seventeenth century, which radically reformed military strategy. Modern weapons systems necessitated hierarchical organization and strict discipline and enabled the instrumentalization of the armed forces for nation-state politics. Warfare was thus monopolized within military institutions. Tendencies towards centralization were reinforced by technological and organizational modernization, boosting efficiency. Military leader-ship took control of the troops' supply, reduced the baggage, and disciplined soldiers. The result is the separation between military and civilian realm, which is taken for granted today. This went hand in hand with the strict gender-specific division of labor that excluded women from most military capacities.

Standardization and disciplining of male soldiers peaked with the mass integration of men into exclusively male conscript armies during the nineteenth century. Conscription inaugurated a new phase of male socialization and constituted the military as a women-free zone. Differences between men were seemingly nullified by their common relationship to state and nation (Kreisky 2003: 4). Warfare was no longer restricted to a caste of warriors—all men became potential soldiers. Military service changed from a profession to a citizen's duty. It provided the basis for rights to political participation, which became dependent on the ability to bear arms and thus on being male. Nationalist perspectives on the state, which became a dominant influence in the nineteenth century, equated political with military participation. The "nation in arms" became a male space (Hagemann 1999: 18). The military therefore represents more than one male institution among others; it is the central "school of the (male) nation" (Kreisky 2003: 6).

Myths of the "masculinity" of war must be understood in the context of these political and military transformations that sharpened gender differences and hierarchies (Hagemann 1999) and established women's roles in the no- or low-income spheres of the military (nurses, administrative staff, wives and mothers of soldiers, volunteer relief workers, advocates of war on the "home front"). As a key institution in modern warfare and modern nation-states, the military became a "male-defining institution"; stereotypes of men as aggressive and courageous became increasingly accepted as ideals for civilian masculinity as well (Stiehm 1988: 3). Compatible images of women as peaceful and vulnerable evolved to complement these masculine ideals.

In the US, similar patterns of professionalization and centralization were at work. Here, too, these processes successively excluded women and disseminated the concept of war as a male endeavor. Compared to Europe, however, the centralization process of the state was less pronounced and also less dependent on military consolidation. Territorial gains played a less significant role in state-formation because there was no comparable competition from neighboring territorial states. Throughout the first centuries of US history, armed conflict mainly involved decentralized confrontations with the indigenous population. Larger military endeavors such as the War of Independence were led by centralized armies, but did not culminate in the establishment of permanent forces. Military organization was long based on state militias. In the anti-statist and federalist tradition of the revolution, a state-controlled military was deemed detrimental to national security. The armed citizens were responsible for protecting the country and also had to be prepared to defend themselves against the state. A separation of military and police tasks first developed with the growing global influence of the US at the turn from the nineteenth to the twentieth century. Until the Second World War, warfare was based on fast mobilization for interventions and sub-sequent demobilization. Technological, social, and geo-political conditions required a standing army only in the second half of the twentieth century. The idealization of aggressive, war-prone masculinity, which also accompanied state-formation in the US, was not based on mass integration into the military apparatus. Here, the predominant image was of the individualistic male pioneer fighting for the ideals of freedom and independence on the Western Frontier. Note, how-ever, that even the frontier society was far from a women-free zone. While conscription was employed to mobilize for interventions, it remained disputed in the context of the voluntaristic and individualist founding ideals of the US. Accordingly, military interventions were less often justified by references to the state than to US values and beliefs.

Women were first formally excluded from US warfare with the founding of the Continental Army, which coordinated the militias of the British colonies during the War of Independence. Despite this formal exclusion from the regular troops, they still officially took part in military activities as nurses or in separate auxiliary units (Murnane 2007). The tradition of exclusion was less rigid and the gender-specific division of military labor was more fluid than in the European conscript armies. The final centralization of military power in unified armed forces after the Second World War, however, led to a stricter exclusion, even though women were now integrated into the regular troops through the Women's Armed Services Integration Act 1948. In the newly established permanent forces, which were no longer based on short-term mobilization, women became part of the peacetime military and fluctuations in their representation were lowered. However, legal limitations on their quantitative and qualitative participation hindered their advancement within the institutions for decades to come.

Though this step made women part of the forces and thus formally constituted "integration," it severely limited women's roles and cut their quantitative representation. With this act, Congress excluded them from combat aircraft and naval vessels and authorized the services to limit women's participation to occupations they saw fit. These measures enabled limited and unequal integration and at the same time sharply reduced actual participation (Murnane 2007). The mechanized, but not yet technologically advanced, military could draw on enough men qualified for military service. The supply of and demand for female labor was low. The "masculinity" of warfare was therefore constitutive for the founding of the modern US military after 1945. These historically grown relations between state, war, and masculinity have evolved in different contexts in Europe and the US. In both cases, they were strongest when military power was consolidated and centralized, i.e. during nation-state formation in Europe and during the US rise to global power. The relation between the state and men, mediated through the military, was in both cases fostered by social, economic, and technological conditions. The result was the definition of war-prone masculinity as a state-supporting ideal, accompanied by the establishment of dichotomized gender ideologies that idealized peaceful femininity.

These developments cannot be separated from economic centralization and industrialization of production, which shaped patterns of gender-specific division of labor in the civilian realm as well. The emergence of industrial capitalism contributed to the dynamism of nation-state formation and helped industrialize warfare. It also played a major role in separating "female" housework and "male" wage labor, setting the stage for ideological gender antagonisms. By defining male and female spheres, emerging labor markets made gender roles more dualistic and labor division more rigid than in pre-industrial times[11]:

> [F]amilies went from the relatively fluid sexual division of labor character-istic of pre-industrial America to the sharp dichotomy between men's and women's spheres that arose as the "important" work of society left the home.
> (Margolis 2000: 80)

The separation of domestic and professional spheres, and the outsourcing of many areas of production that had been conducted by women and men cooperatively into smaller and then larger factories, left women with the remaining tasks of child-rearing, food preparation, and house work[12]:

> [T]he American family, once a unit that both produced and consumed goods, became a unit of consumption alone. Prior to industrialization, much of what was produced was the responsibility of the housewife whose work was far more varied and crucial to her family's survival. ... [M]en, women, and children worked side by side in and around the household. As such, there was

little distinction between "work" and "life," so that women did not have to choose between "work" and "staying home" as alternative careers.

(Margolis 2000: 71)

Economic change transformed the definitions and functions of the family, making it a central institution for the socialization of future and regeneration of current workers within industrialized economy. Additionally, the new definition of "female" tasks connected the work of the housewife and mother to the well-being of society and the nation. In the emerging consumerist society of twentieth-century USA, gendered labor division and associated ideological formations fulfilled important economic functions: they provided the basis for maximizing the private consumption on which the US economy increasingly depended. The nuclear family and the dependent housewife were therefore central to the functioning of industrial capitalism:

> [T]he core of housework in the twentieth-century America is buying goods and preparing them for family use ... . Without the free services of the housewife, the expansion of household consumption—critical to the growth of the American economy in the twentieth century—would have been sharply curtailed.

(Margolis 2000: 84)

Female employment rates were low under these circumstances, particularly among married, American-born women from the growing middle classes. From the second half of the nineteenth-century, immigrants from Europe provided cheap labor and unions campaigned against women's employment. Men's wages were high enough to support the hegemonic family model only without competition from cheap female labor and with cost-free housework: "The wage and salary structure of industrial capitalism was—and still is—dependent on the child care, cooking, and cleaning done gratis by women" (ibid.: 83). Middle-class women were not only not required on labor markets, but their work in organizing consumption and in educating future workforce generations was crucial for maintaining the existing social order.

The twin-forces of socio-economic and military change transformed the gender-specific division of labor in the civilian and the military realm. In Europe and North America these structural developments led to the idealization of war-prone masculinity and established the military as a site of male initiation rites. The soldier became the ideal type and embodiment of masculinity (Morgan 1994: 165). The symbolic relevance of the "protection of women" as a legitimization for military activity and the construction of women as valuable possessions of men (Seifert 1996: 180ff.) were also effects of transformations that can be traced back to the nineteenth century. Since then, women, their protection, or freedom have often been cited as the "true reasons" for going to war. At the same time they have also been blamed for obstructing the war effort in case of defeat (Albrecht-Heide 1988: 118f.). Female victims of war do not question this "protection myth," even though the unharmed female body symbolizes male power.[13] The image of women as peaceful and nurturing, as instrumentalized within anti-war movements (Cockburn 1998), is also an expression of these social and military structures. Due to the historical connection between war and masculinity, military gender ideologies are applied beyond the borders of the biologically defined sexes. The masculinization of fighting women, feminization of the enemy (Enloe 1990) or of anti-war activists and deserters (Gray 1959), as well as both forms of gendering of groups, nations, and events are common phenomena in wartime.

The ideological dichotomy between peaceful women and aggressive men can be explained by examining the social and military conditions under which both sexes were incorporated into social and military structures and institutions. These conditions determine the functions of gender images in regard to war and the military. Separation of domestic and wage labor, the establishment of the bourgeois family model in industrial capitalism, as well as centralization and militarization of warfare represent the context within which military gender stereotypes have emerged in the US at the turn of the twentieth century. As these conditions changed, so did the images and their functionality.

Rationalization and professionalization of the US military: the roots of women's integration

The historical perspective helps explain the constitution of the military as a "male" institution and highlights the multiple causes of women's exclusion. This institutionalization of masculinity also provides the historical background from which processes of military gender integration emanated in the second half of the twentieth century. In this time period, the heightened rationalization and professionalization of production and warfare initiated a major turn in gender-specific labor division, one that integrated women into civilian and military labor markets. Patterns of labor division changed radically, especially from the 1970s onwards when middle-class women increasingly entered the job market and feminist movements supported positive attitudes towards this new independence. At the same time, military labor markets were revolutionized by the abolishment of the draft and the establishment of the All-Volunteer Force. This double integration provided the foundation for the changes in military gender ideologies during the period of investigation. Both processes were deeply intertwined and depended on technological advancement and rationalization, initiating complex interactions between them. The following chapter more closely examines these interactions to identify the various factors that enabled military gender integration and continue to influence it.

A main precondition for integration was the change of military personnel requirements in the course of organizational and strategic reform. The advanced technology and professionalization in both the civilian and military sectors had profound direct and indirect effects on military institutions and their personnel. They affected quantitative and qualitative personnel demands, but also changed the personnel supply by triggering similar processes on civilian labor markets.

Advanced technology changed demands on the individual by marginalizing physical strength as a criterion for military service. It also changed the organization of warfare by increasing the ratio of supply, support, and administration units in relation to combat troops (Segal 1995: 762). Military organizations diversified. While some areas remained traditionally organized, such as ground combat troops, others converged with the civilian realm, especially in administrative and technical areas (Janowitz 1965; Moskos 1973). Boundaries between military and civilian sectors became more fluid compared to their rather rigid separation before the Second World War:

> Prior to World War II, there were important differences between civilian and military organizations, between the military and civilian work forces, and between military service and civilian employment. There were crucial technological differences between the two spheres, rooted in the fact that military and civilian personnel spent their time doing different things.
>
> (Segal/Segal 1983: 160)

Before the Second World War, US warfare had been a land-based activity, in which the infantry represented the military's core (Segal/Segal 1983: 151ff.). Most recruits were mobilized for interventions and demobilized shortly thereafter. Changing technological and strategic conditions redefined the mission, emphasizing deterrent and peace-keeping tasks. "[A]s technology deprived nations of the lead time required to mobilize for war from a small base" (ibid.: 161) it became impossible to rely on short-term mobilization of recruits. As a result, the "distinction between peacetime and wartime became less relevant for military organizations" (ibid.). The US established a large force of about two million troops or 1 percent of the population, which was maintained in peacetime (Segal/Segal 2004: 4f.). Specialized, better qualified non-combat personnel were increasingly required, also on lower ranks, due to rising complexity of equipment and growing proportion of support units (Riche 2005: 23; Warner and Asch 2001: 174).

With increased professionalization and "civilization" of some military tasks, the random draft of young men before higher education became inefficient, because the average educational level of young adults dropped beneath military requirements. These structural transformations were the main reasons for abolishing conscription and introducing the All-Volunteer Force (AVF) in 1973, marking a shift from a partly to a completely professionalized US Armed Forces.[14] The unpopularity of the long-lasting Vietnam War, along with the onus of defeat, facilitated that change: it weakened traditional military elites and provided space for liberalization and the formation of social movements (Niva 1998: 115). The abolition of the conscript military, however, cannot be attributed solely to the impact of the Vietnam War as a singular event, but has its roots in broader social and military processes.

Reorganization in a volunteer force boosted the average level of qualification and education of recruits. The draft had generated more recruits with highest scores in qualification tests than the AVF, but even more with the lowest (Warner/ Asch 2001: 181). This shift also reduced the number of troops and training costs without reducing readiness. The fluctuation of personnel sank and thus the yearly demand for new recruits (ibid.: 170f.).[15] Trained and experienced personnel could be retained in the service longer. This made better qualified personnel and increasingly expensive military technology affordable (ibid.: 175). The proportion of personnel costs within the defense budget sank,[16] while expenditures for equipment, research, and development rose (ibid.: 177).

The transition to the AVF made the military the largest employer in the US (Segal/Segal 2004: 5), a labor market in itself, that followed patterns similar to its civilian counterpart. Though the volunteer force better suited the personnel requirements of modernized warfare, it also complicated recruitment. Military organizations now had to compete with civilian employers (Riche 2005: 1) because they "began to require personnel with skills that were also needed in the civilian economy" (Segal/Segal 1983: 161). White middle-class men, who had made up the majority of the draft military, could no longer be conscripted, and the more qualified they were, the more often they preferred civilian employment. "High ability individuals" who acquired the highest scores in the Armed Forces Qualification Test (AFQT) and had high-school degrees were more likely to go to college than join the military (Kleykamp 2006: 277). Professionalization on civilian labor markets had generally increased the average level of education because the civilian economy also needed a better qualified workforce. Increased rates of college enrolment, however, reduced the pool of potential recruits. More young people possessed the qualification level required by the military, but were also better qualified for the civilian labor market (Riche 2005: 3f.).

Rising qualification requirements and competition with the civilian labor market impeded recruitment. From the mid-1970s to the mid-1980s the military required 300,000 new recruits each year to sustain an active force of 1.8 million troops (Armor and Gilroy 2007: 7). It thus became more dependent on groups that were discriminated against on the labor market and therefore easier to recruit. The demographic make-up of military personnel was transformed, particularly of enlisted troops who comprise about 85 percent of all personnel (Riche 2005: 1). Though the military recruits few from the lowest (or the highest) social classes (Segal and Segal 2004: 24), young people joining the military were increasingly likely to be characterized by low family income, low educational level of parents, and having a rural background in the South (Kleykamp 2006: 277).

The change in social make-up went hand in hand with the altered ethnic composition of the military. African-American men became the most likely to enter military service. Within the first five years of the AVF, blacks' representation rose from 14 percent to 19 percent. Between 1976 and 1980 their percentage in the Army increased from 24 percent to 33 percent, in the Marine Corps from 17 percent to 22 percent (Armor/Gilroy 2007: 4). From the early 1980s onwards the value was around 22 percent of all enlisted personnel and 30 percent of enlisted Army members (Warner/Asch 2001: 185). The corresponding levels are

21 percent of the Navy, 18 percent of the Air Force, and 15 percent of the Marines (Segal and Segal 2004: 20). When compared to blacks' representation among the general population, these numbers show a strong relationship between social status, race, and the propensity to enlist. African-Americans are particularly overrepresented on the lowest ranks and among personnel assigned to the most dangerous jobs (Stiehm 1996: 65) such as active ground combat (Armor 1996: 20). Minority overrepresentation among applicants for military service is even higher. Qualification requirements and associated recruitment and assignment practices, however, reduce this proportion because young people from minority populations are less likely to have a high-school degree and have lower average results in qualification tests (ibid.: 15). Their disadvantaged status on civilian labor markets is reflected in the positive correlation between civilian unemployment and African-American military representation: The tenser the market, the more blacks enter military service (Armor and Gilroy 2007: 10).

Cross-national comparison (Segal 1995) reveals that the degree of technological advancement of equipment and the combat-to-support ratio strongly influence women's military participation. If increased demand for qualified personnel cannot be met with male recruits, shortages are compensated for by integrating women. The transition to the AVF has thus significantly changed the gender-specific division of military labor. Though women had been part of the armed forces before, their participation reached new quantitative and qualitative levels after the draft was abolished. From 1972 to the mid-1980s, the percentage increased from under 2 percent to approximately 9 percent (Table 3.1). The more sophisticated recruitment requirements made women's participation a necessity to maintain quality standards (Riche 2005: 16f.). Technological modernization promoted this: physical strength had lost relevance as a requirement for military service, and weapons technology facilitated women's participation (Binkin 1986). More importantly, technology had great impact upon military organization: Ever more personnel worked in occupations which required similar qualifications to the civilian sector. More women possessed the physical preconditions for military service, even in combat positions, and they provided the much needed qualified personnel for the growing support structure. Under these conditions, military interventions raised female representation. This is because most military women are part of the reserves, which are mobilized in the case of war. In wartime, the proportion of support units is higher than in peacetime (Segal 1995: 765; Iskra 2007: 773).

The factors behind women's integration went beyond the transformation of military occupations and the rising need for a qualified workforce. They also included changes in the overall gender-specific division of labor in the civilian economy, which underwent the same rationalization process as the military:

Trends toward rationalization in modern society have been reflected in the American armed forces in bureaucratization and in increasing concerns with professionalism, management, and the cash nexus that links the serviceperson to the military. These trends are common in the corporate world as well. Thus in one sense the military can be seen not as a unique institution but rather as a laboratory in which widespread social processes can be observed.

(Segal and Segal 1983: 165)

Technological advancement and professionalization of occupations has redefined both, civilian and military labor markets in the USA since the 1950s. The growth

Table 3.1 Proportion and quantity of female active duty personnel 1970–2005

Year	Female active duty personnel (%)	Female active duty personnel (numbers)	Total active duty personnel
1970	1.4	41,479	3,064,760
1971	1.6	42,775	2,713,044
1972	1.9	45,033	2,321,959
1973	2.5	55,402	2,251,936
1974	3.5	74,715	2,162,005
1975	4.5	96,868	2,128,120
1976	5.2	109,133	2,081,910
1977	5.7	118,966	2,074,543
1978	6.5	134,312	2,061,708
1979	7.5	151,082	2,026,892
1980	8.4	171,418	2,050,627
1981	8.9	184,651	2,082,560
1982	9.0	189,048	2,108,612
1983	9.3	197,878	2,123,349
1984	9.5	202,830	2,138,157
1985	9.8	211,606	2,151,032
1986	10.0	218,889	2,169,112
1987	10.2	223,805	2,174,217
1988	10.5	224,836	2,138,213
1989	10.9	232,823	2,130,229
1990	11.1	227,018	2,043,705
1991	11.1	221,138	1,985,555
1992	11.6	210,048	1,807,177
1993	11.9	203,506	1,705,103
1994	12.3	199,688	1,610,490
1995	12.9	196,116	1,518,224
1996	13.4	197,693	1,471,722
1997	13.9	200,526	1,438,562
1998	14.1	198,420	1,406,830
1999	14.5	200,287	1,385,703
2000	14.6	202,601	1,384,338
2001	14.9	207,188	1,385,116
2002	15.0	212,266	1,411,634
2003	15.0	215,243	1,434,377
2004	14.9	212,156	1,426,836
2005	14.6	202,949	1,389,394

Source: Department of Defense: Selected Manpower Statistics Fiscal Year 2005

of the service sector in relation to industrial production is the socio-economic equivalent of the transition of the conscript to the volunteer military. This process supported women's integration on civilian labor markets, in turn making their qualifications more attractive to the military. Although the military had depended on women in areas that were dominated by them in the civilian realm (e.g. health care) even before the 1970s, women were now qualified for a wider range of military occupations. A general rule is that the higher women's civilian labor market participation, the higher their military representation (Segal 1995: 766f.). Again, not only quantitative, but also qualitative aspects are relevant. Less segregated labor markets opened more opportunities to women in the military: "[S]ex segregation in the civilian labor market is negatively related to women's military participation" (Segal 1999: 568). Convergence of civilian and military occupations and of male and female occupations raised the probability with which women possess relevant qualifications for military service.

Rising female employment rates originated in the transformation of the US economy, which increased supply of and demand for a female workforce. After World War II, US industry shifted its focus to the production of consumer goods. Due to stable markets and high consumption rates, military industry could easily adapt to peace-time conditions. Increased extension of loans raised the ability to consume (and the indebtedness) of large parts of the population (Margolis 2000: 97ff.). At the same time, the service sector grew in relation to industrial and agricultural production, reducing male wages and increasing growth in branches in which female participation was high. As an effect of stagnating industrial goods markets, this tertiary sector finally became the domineering economic sphere in the 1970s. Professional structures were effectively changed due to a strong decrease in employees in agricultural production, but also in industry, handicraft, and trade. Many of the newly developed jobs in service provided only low income (Prokop 2001: 381). These "larger shifts in the nation's occupational structure from one based on manual and blue-collar labor before World War II to service and white-collar labor in the postwar years" (Margolis 2000: 146) increased the demand for a workforce in traditionally female occupations and made high levels of consumption dependent on female income: "In short, women's expanded role in the workforce reflected both greater demand for their labor and increased need for their earnings in a consumption-driven economy" (ibid.: 147).

These processes have enhanced women's employment and at the same time created gender-specific segregation on labor markets in that women tend to dominate in disadvantaged occupations. As a result, separate labor markets for men and women have evolved (Oppenheimer 1970). Women were mainly employed in certain areas of "white-collar labor" in which most jobs were temporary, part time, and with little career prospects. They required little investment from employers because necessary qualifications were mostly acquired prior to employment. Moreover, most women worked within branches in which employees were less often unionized and therefore cheaper. This is one reason why it became more profitable for the private sector to invest in the production of services than in the production of goods (Margolis 2000: 146ff.). As a consequence, the overall make-up of the female workforce, which had long consisted mainly of industrial workers, changed. In 1960, the labor market participation of middle-class women reached 50 percent. While many professional women from the middle classes were young and unmarried during the 1940s, the average age of the female workforce was 41 years by the mid-1950s (ibid.: 145). Women's and men's career patterns began to converge: more women worked year-round, fulltime, and after the birth of children. Market changes also transformed family patterns. Rising costs of living and inflation and high female employment decreased birth rates and increased marital age (ibid.: 61f.), delayed the foundation of a family, and reduced the average number of children. These developments also facilitated women's military integration (Segal 1996: 768).

The erosion of the structures that had supported the model of the male wage earner and the dependent wife and mother were accompanied by a change of values. Gender ideologies redefined men's and women's roles as parents and partners as well as responsibilities within the national economy. Feminism expressed these material transformations and openly questioned the bourgeois family ideal:

> Consumerism, inflation, falling male wages, and an increase in demand for labor in female occupations all created a virtual revolution in women's employment activities. As more and more wives and mothers went to work and as the two-income family became standard, a great awakening occurred ... Spurred on by feminism, a movement that was itself partly a response to the reality of work in women's lives, women's domestic advisors, public opinion, and the popular media belatedly acknowledged that perhaps women's place was not really in the home.
>
> (Margolis 2000: 152)

Hierarchical gender dichotomies did, however, not completely dissolve after the 1960s. Selective participation on labor markets is still supported by notions of gender-specific abilities and entitlements. The professional world remains gender segregated, even though more and more women work in male-dominated areas. Their belated entry into the civilian labor market under discriminatory conditions continues to be expressed in lower wages and dominance in "female" occupations. This discrimination yields precisely the kind of workforce that the professionalized military increasingly demands: a reserve of low-cost, qualified non-combatants. Both labor markets are thus not only structured by similar patterns of gender integration—they stand in a reciprocal relationship to each other, with gender-specific effects. Overall, this interaction has facilitated or even enabled integration. More women are now better qualified for military service, but still benefit less than men from better qualifications on civilian labor markets. This is also expressed in the positive correlation between male unemployment and female military participation. During the late 1970s and early 1980s, female participation rates dropped, when male unemployment was high. When enough civilian jobs were available to men, the proportion of women in the military rose (Segal 1995: 767). Low wages, high unemployment, and high inflation increase the military's personnel supply and lower women's participation. Their opportunities increase in tense labor markets, when men prefer better paying jobs in the civilian economy (Iskra 2007: 767; Warner and Asch 2001: 168). This dynamic affects military participation of all groups that are discriminated against on civilian labor markets. Heightened competition thereon increases the integration of marginalized groups into the military.

For women, the intersection between gender, race, and social class can lead to double and even triple discrimination. In the AVF, minorities are generally overrepresented, but minority women are even more so. African-American women are the most likely group of women to join the military, followed by Hispanic and white women. They are particularly overrepresented among enlisted ranks, where blacks account for 20 percent of male, but 34 percent of female troops (Warner/Asch 2001: 185). Women with only one parent or whose parents have no college degree are also overrepresented. Those with children are more likely to join the military than go to college. At the same time, social background and educational level are less influential on women's propensity to enlist than on men's (Segal *et al.* 1986). This underscores that women do not benefit from higher educational levels on the civilian labor market to the same extent as men.

Downsizing and gender equality: the 1990s and beyond

Considering past and current processes of gender integration, a set of social and military factors can be identified that affect women's military participation. Military personnel requirements directly influence the quantity and quality of integration. These requirements are in turn determined by broader socio-economic processes that transform military organization. Military recruiting cannot be analyzed solely in terms of personnel demands. The supply side has to be taken into account as well in order to understand personnel policies and appendant gender-specific inclusions and exclusions. This approach enables examining relations between the military and its socio-economic, demographic, and technological environments, which are influential on gender integration and thus on gender ideology. The following chapter more closely highlights these relations during the period of investigation.

During the 1970s, social and military changes created the basis for women's enhanced military service. Only in the 1990s, however, the conditions arose for a substantial quantitative and qualitative change of their roles. A strong increase in participation and an implementation of comprehensive equality measures were the results. From a military perspective, two developments were decisive for the time period:

First, the end of the Cold War coupled with budget constraints has led to a substantial restructuring and downsizing of our military forces. These force reductions require special personnel policies and decisions in the areas of recruiting and reenlistment that can affect race and gender representation. Second, the Persian Gulf War was the first large-scale military action after conversion to an all-volunteer force.

(Armor 1996: 8)

The introduction of the AVF had institutionalized a large, permanent peacetime military whose personnel levels were kept high by the Cold War. With the end of the bloc confrontation, personnel downsizing began, which was only retained for the Persian Gulf War in 1991 and the interventions in Afghanistan and Iraq (Segal/Segal 2004: 4). Active troops now required around 200,000 new recruits and 15,000 to 20,000 new officers each year (ibid.: 8). Quantitatively, personnel requirements were decreasing. The US military became much smaller in terms of manpower, but it also became technologically more advanced. The ongoing trends of technologization and professionalization had been further promoted by the military build-up of the 1980s (Mariscal 1991: 106). The workforce was reduced, but qualification requirements kept rising, so that the average level of education remained below what the military considered necessary to join the forces (Riche 2005: 23). The Pentagon required a minimum of 90 percent of enlisted personnel in each service to have a high-school degree and 60 percent to reach over 50 percent in the AFQT. Recruits with scores in the lowest category fell beneath 10 percent in the 1980s and have since 1991 accounted for only 1 percent to 2 percent of personnel. A slight increase was observed in 2005, when recruitment for the Iraq intervention became increasingly difficult (Armor/Gilroy 2007: 10).

Average AFQT results improved and high-school degrees, which only two thirds of recruits had possessed in 1973, became more widespread among the general population, since higher education also became more important on the civilian labor market. The proportion of young adults between 25 and 29 who obtained four or more years of college rose from 21 percent in 1974 to 29 percent in 2004 (Warner and Asch 2001: 181). Note, however, that the general rise in US's average educational levels brought little improvement for younger cohorts, mostly due to the large-scale immigration of young populations with low levels of education. During the 1990s, still only 30 percent to 35 percent of candidates were eligible for military service (Stiehm 1996: 65); only 50 percent of these actually joined the military (Angrist 1995: 2). While the average education level rose among young Americans, it was still beneath the military's requirements.

Professionalization and rationalization have since been a double-edged sword in terms of recruitment conditions. Though competition with civilian employers has impeded recruitment of enough qualified personnel, increasing qualification requirements in the professionalized service economy also opened new opportunities for recruitment. Combined with rising costs for education, stagnating family incomes, and limited student grants, the enhanced relevance of higher education became a recruitment asset. Though high-school graduates are more likely to go to college than join the military, the decreased affordability of higher education is now used to attract youth from lower and middle classes to the military (ibid.: 6). Since education costs have grown faster than family incomes during the 1990s, the military is not merely competing with colleges, but also represents a way for many young Americans to get there (Kleykamp 2006: 274f.). Military service enables the transition to further education and to civilian jobs. In many cases, military careers no longer parallel civilian ones, but supplement them: military service often precedes entering the civilian labor market and enhances opportunities thereon (Riche 2005: 10ff.). Compared to service in the draft military, which tended to reduce future civilian incomes of conscripts, the AVF offers a certain degree of social mobility, caused by educational benefits (Angrist 1995: 1; Kleykamp 2006: 272). These enhanced opportunities have also been promoted because military and civilian jobs have become more alike and many qualifications acquired in the former can be easily transferred to the latter.

While higher qualification requirements account for qualitative recruitment problems, demographic changes in the population's age-structure helped reduce the quantity of potential recruits. If the youth population declines in relation to the size of the military, and retention rates remain stable, recruitment can become problematic (Armor/Gilroy 2007: 7). Low birth rates aggravated the generally tense recruitment situation during the 1990s and beyond, despite personnel downsizing. The population growth initiated by the Baby Boom began to stall during the 1990s and the proportion of young adults decreased in relation to the general population. These conditions furthered women's integration, but also affected the representation of social and ethnic groups that are disadvantaged on civilian labor markets. Again, military restructuring transformed the demographic make-up of the military population. Minorities had been overrepresented in actual recruits (and even more so in applicants for the AVF) since its outset. This continued into the 1990s. The closing of many military bases in the course of downsizing was also influential: the propensity to enlist is enhanced for those living in areas with high military presence. Military bases are now concentrated in rural, southern, and western areas, where poorer, black, and Hispanic populations are overrepresented (Segal and Segal 2004: 10). Lower qualification levels among minorities still accounted for reduced admission quotas during the 1990s. In 1994, 9 percent of white and 30 percent of black applicants were among those who scored under 30 percent in the AFQT. A proportion of 64 percent of white and 52 percent of black male applicants, as well as 45 percent of white and 38 percent of black female applicants, were enlisted (Armor 1996: 19).

However, during the period investigated here, minority representation began to approximate representation among the general population. The number of African-American troops stabilized in the 1980s and even began to sink in the 1990s (Armor and Gilroy 2007: 1). This can be explained by the increased average educational level among young blacks, which was significant enough to account for the overall rise in US education levels. While the proportion of high-school degree holders had differed for white and black populations until the early 1980s, these numbers began to converge in the mid-1980s. The percentage of African-Americans who hold a degree reached 75 percent, where it remains until today. That rate for whites has increased only slightly from 82 percent to 84 percent during the past 35 years (ibid.: 9). Blacks' opportunities on civilian labor markets were thus enhanced during the 1980s, reducing interest in military careers (Armor 1996: 13). Distribution of black and white recruits on different hierarchy levels of the military also converged. With the increase in black college graduates, the proportion of black officers rose from 3 percent at the beginning of the AVF to 9 percent in 2002. In 1974, only 8 percent of African-Americans had graduated from college, in 2004 17 percent had (Segal and Segal 2004: 20). Differences in AFQT-results were also reduced during the 1990s. While 15 percent of black applicants reached the three highest categories of scores in the 1980s, 26 percent did in 1997 (Armor and Gilroy 2007: 9).

Similar patterns were repeated later and to a lesser degree in the representation of Hispanics. In 1975 their representation was at 2 percent and began to rise only in the 1980s. Their proportion among enlisted personnel reached between 7 percent and 9 percent in the early 1990s and 3.1 percent on officer ranks, while their representation among youth populations had already reached between 13 percent and 15 percent (Warner/Asch 2001: 185; Armor 1996: 16). With growing Hispanic representation among youths and their increased average educational level—55 percent held high-school-degrees in the 1970s, 66 percent did so in 2006; college graduation increased from 5 percent to 11 percent—their military representation rose to 10 percent in 2001 and has begun to slightly decrease since then (Armor/Gilroy 2007: 1; Segal and Segal 2004: 23). Like for African-Americans, Hispanics' representation among the different services negatively correlates with the degree of technologization and associated qualification requirements. Their representation is thus lowest among Air Force personnel (4 percent) and highest among the Marines (15 percent) (Segal and Segal 2004: 23). Hispanic participation is also promoted by immigration policy because military service speeds up the naturalization process. A total of 35,000 active troops and 8,000 reservists are non-citizens (Riche 2005: 13).

The reduced fluctuation of personnel during downsizing altered the demographic make-up of military populations. During the early 1990s, the proportion of enlisted personnel with more than four years of work experience increased to 54 percent (Warner and Asch 2001: 179). The average length of a military career is now 10 years, for officers 20 years (Segal and Segal 2004: 10; Armor 1996: 20). Less fluctuation means a higher average age of personnel. It also means increased competition for promotion to higher ranks. This is because the military follows an up or out policy, which requires personnel to be promoted at regular intervals or leave the service. While promotion on lower ranks is usually automatic after a certain amount of time, applicants for higher ranks compete directly with each other, with the unsuccessful ones required to leave their jobs. This maintains the military's youth[17] and prevents a top-heavy rank structure (Segal and Segal 2004: 10). The 1990s downsizing thus increased competitiveness for promotion, particularly at higher ranks (Stiehm 1996: 56), during a time when women's opportunities in the services were expanded.

Due to changes in age structure and career patterns, military careers in the 1990s and beyond more often overlapped with the foundation of a family. Over half of the military population is married and the rate of marriages between service members is rising (Segal and Segal 2004: 31). Military men in general and military women to the age of 30 are more often married than civilians of the same age and are more likely to have children. More military wives are now working outside the home and more service members are single parents. These trends make personnel more expensive and less flexible. Nonetheless, since the military must maintain high reenlistment rates, it must concern itself with family issues (Riche 2005: 14ff.). Families have become an increasingly powerful factor in the military's considerations because job satisfaction can be negatively affected by family concerns, especially with the high demands that the military poses on families (Segal 1986).

One of the most significant demographic changes in the military population during the 1990s was the increase in female service members. After the first strong ascent with the introduction of the AVF (from under 2 percent in 1972 to around 11 percent in the 1980s), and a period of stagnation between 1983 and 1991 with only a slight increase after the implementation of the "risk rule" in 1988, a major rise in representation came in the early 1990s (Table 3.1). In 1995, 18 percent of personnel enlisted were female (Armor 1996: 12ff.). Due to recruitment shortages caused by rising qualification requirements, low birth rates, and falling minority representation, women's participation was widened. Many barriers were lifted, while some discriminations, such as the exclusion from ground combat, sub-marines, and Special Forces, remained in place. This artificial reduction of demand for a female workforce make women who enter military service on average higher qualified than men (Warner and Asch 2001: 187). The percentage has now stabilized around 15 percent of active troops. In September 2005, 14 percent of active Army personnel (70,454 of 492,728), 14 percent of Navy personnel (52,381 of 362,942), 19.5 percent of the Air Force (69,151 of 353,696) and 6 percent of the Marines (10,963 of 180,029) were women. This corresponds to around 203,000 of 1.4 million active duty personnel (Brown 2006: 2). During the 1970s, personnel supply and demand were the key factors behind both women's integration and its limitation. With increased female representation in the services, the flexibility of personnel management in assigning and deploying women increasingly became an issue (Iskra 2007: 214).

Again, we must look beyond the military to account for changes in the gendered military labor division during the 1990s and after. The military is embedded within general social processes and thus also influenced by them. One important factor is the gendered labor division in the civilian sector. The quantity and quality of women's employment rates are strong indicators for their military integration. During the 1990s, the service sector expanded and strengthened its proportional dominance; this caused growth in occupational areas, in which women were over-represented. Women's employment rates thus increased, while gender-specific segregation of occupations and discrimination persisted. Women still dominated in traditionally female, lower paying jobs of medium quality. In the early twenty-first century, 80 percent of working women were employed in only 20 percent of the 420 professional fields listed by the Department of Labor. At the same time, they had to make an extra effort to maintain family income because the wages of 80 percent of men had been sinking since the 1970s (Margolis 2000: 149f.). In 1975, men earned more than 60 percent of family incomes in 77 percent of households. In 2000, only 58 percent of households fell into this category, while the percentage of households in which both partners earned approximately the same rose from 17 percent to 29 percent (Riche 2005: 12).

Gender-based discrimination on civilian labor markets still intersects with social status and ethnic background such that the female military population is ethnically more diverse than that in the civilian workforce. Half of military women are non-Caucasian, while only one quarter of working civilian women are (Williams 2005). African-American women are more strongly overrepresented in the military than African-American men: 34 percent of enlisted females, but only 20 percent of males, are black. The equivalent values among officers are 16 percent and 9 percent. African-American women account for one quarter of female officers and half of enlisted women. Latinas account for 4 percent of female officers and 10 percent of enlisted women (Segal/Segal 2004: 30).

Gender policies as reactions to changing recruitment conditions

Legal and military personnel policies have adapted the role of women to the social and military conditions of recruitment and gender policies were implemented to regulate participation according to military needs. These patterns already existed prior to the abolishment of conscription. Throughout military history, legal conditions have enabled at least temporary deployment of women, when it was required (Segal 1995: 761). Until 1948, women were assigned to special auxiliary units established in cases of personnel shortages (Peach 1996: 157). The Second World War saw the quantitatively largest participation in US military interventions, but was followed by the most rigid exclusionary policies. The Women's Armed Services Integration Act of 1948 made women regular members of the peacetime military and at the same time limited their participation. This handicapped advancement for decades (Segal 1995: 761). Women's proportion was restricted to a maximum of 2 percent until 1967; promotion beyond certain ranks and assignment to combat ships and aircraft were forbidden by law. As no rules concerning ground combat were included in the bill, it was left to the services to prevent involvement in direct combat. Each service was legitimized to formulate their own regulations on integration (Murnane 2007: 1068; Titunik 2000: 243).

The Armed Services Integration Act has since served as an efficient tool to shape integration according to military needs. Its double function has concurrently both promoted and limited integration. This was mostly achieved by changing the definitions of "combat." During the 1950s and 1960s, the bill was amended several times to grant the military more flexibility in assigning and deploying women (Iskra 2007: 208). The 2 percent quota was already lifted in 1967, when the Vietnam War caused personnel shortages (Peach 1996: 158), and military academies and pilot training were opened to women in 1976. The increased dependency on women's labor changed the nature of integration and associated policies. The Equal Rights Amendment of 1972 was an acknowledgement of a stronger dependency on the female workforce in the civilian sector and also enhanced women's self-consciousness within the military. It also became the legal basis on which military women demanded equality in the workplace from the government and enforced access to military academies and benefits for their dependents (Iskra 2007: 204).

With the rising number of qualified women and the reform of gender policy in the civilian realm, integration measures became connected to the issue of gender equality. Increasing numbers and growing self-esteem gave rise to organizations that protected military women's interests and successfully enforced their demands. The Defense Advisory Committee on Women in the Services (DACOWITS), already established in 1951 to attract female recruits, became a powerful institution that put gender issues such as sexual harassment on the military leadership's agenda (Gabbert 2007: 212). From the late 1970s, the committee engaged in activities to enhance equality in the services, a task that had taken place outside of the feminist movement until very recently (Titunik 2000: 245): "The women's liberation movement, however, which could have been a relevant force, has largely ignored the military" (Thomas 1978: 643).

With the standardization of the formerly different rules on women's participation in 1988, the Pentagon introduced the "risk rule" that opened positions in combat support (Brown 2006: 10f.). When women reached a certain proportion among personnel, flexibility of personnel management became decisive (Iskra 2007: 214). Due to the reasons outlined above, new regulations were introduced in the 1990s that widened women's roles. But even with the lifting of many assignment bans, the Integration Act continued to function as an instrument to limit participation to the military's requirements. Female service members were thus restrained to areas in which they were needed: mostly non-combat specialities in support and supply units on lower and middle salary levels. The remaining "combat exclusion" is crucial to women's status as service members because it prevents qualifying for leadership positions that are legally open (Harrell/Miller 1997: xvii). These limitations constitute de facto quotas that reduce representation, even though all services officially abolished gender quotas in the 1990s.

While social and military conditions and developments provide the basis for integration, the process itself is shaped by various groups of social, military, and political actors which pursue different interests during military restructuring. Laws and internal personnel policies are primarily reactions to the above-mentioned conditions which determine the success or failure of politicians' and civil society organizations' initiatives for and against gender integration. Nonetheless, rules and regulations can considerably shape integration and initiate new dynamics. Political leadership and its gender policy agendas can strongly restrain the military's autonomy. Changes in political power relations are therefore relevant to the gender-specific labor division in the military. Commitment of the ruling party to gender equality in the civilian realm can favor the implementation of new rules and procedures that advance military integration. It is no coincidence that the major changes in military gender policy during the 1990s took place under Democratic rule. In this phase, a connection was drawn between military requirements and gender equality that not only enabled adapting women's roles to personnel needs, but also promoted equal rights within the services. Note, however, that Republican rule with its more conservative stance on gender policy cannot be generally equated with suppression or degradation of military women. First steps in the integration process of the 1990s were already taken by the Bush Senior administration. Despite anti-feminist rhetoric, it was also not reversed during the presidency of George W. Bush. However, the relationship between integration and equality was loosened and military imperatives were given more weight than democratic citizenship standards. Initiatives inside and outside the military have also affected the situation and contributed to the dynamic of change. Military institutionalizations of women's interests, such as DACOWITS, were able to exert great influence on expanding roles (Bellafair 2006). Opponents of integration, such as conservative women's groups, also shaped integration processes with their resistance against gender equality in the services.

The Services

The different branches of the Armed Services have experienced uneven integration. According to their personnel structure and tasks, the transition to a volunteer force and the legal expansion of women's possibilities in the 1990s differently impacted each branch. These gender-related differences also document the relationship between differentiation of military tasks, labor division, and integration. Generally, women's participation varies according to the degree of technologization and the combat-to-support ratio. A high proportion of qualified jobs on lower and middle ranks and low proportion of (ground) combat troops usually enhance representation. Due to varied personnel needs, each service pursues different integration policies within the framework of legal constraints and thus propagates gender ideologies that relate to its specific personnel requirements.

The Army was the only service that drafted recruits before the introduction of the AVF. It is also the largest force, requires the most new recruits each year, and at the same time lacks demand for its jobs. Consequently, the Army was most directly affected by the end of the draft. After failed attempts to reinstall conscription, its readiness to assign women and present them as an integral part of the institution was higher than in other services (Brown 2006: 4). From the early 1970s, the Army aimed recruitment campaigns directly at women and depicted itself as a pioneer of gender equality. In 1978 the separate Women's Corps were dissolved and its former members integrated into the regular units. Since the Army's support structure is relatively large, female participation has always been high. Even before Secretary of Defense Les Aspin rescinded the "risk rule," the Army had made comprehensive plans to extend women's roles (Asch *et al.* 2001: 17f.). Aspin's new policy opened over 32,000 jobs to women (WREI n.d.), and between 1992 and 1995 representation among enlisted personnel increased from 16 percent to 19 percent (Armor 1996: 14).

At the same time, the Army's preoccupation with ground combat limits the participation of women: it reduces demand for qualified personnel and maintains legal boundaries on integration in many areas, even after the expansion of opportunities in the 1990s. Twenty-two percent of female officers and 25 percent of enlisted personnel serve in combat support. Most Army women—72 percent on officer and 74 percent on enlisted ranks—serve in traditionally female occupations such as administration and medical care (Asch *et al.* 2001: 20). While open to expand roles in combat support positions, Army leadership has continuously spoken out against lifting the ban on ground combat. Rules on co-location that forbid stationing women in support with combat troops remained unspecific to retain maximum flexibility in the deployment of support units. When enough male personnel were available, they were interpreted more strictly than the law required (Harrell and Miller 1997: 13). During the "War on Terror" they were laid out more generously to prevent shortages.

The Navy never drafted recruits, but with the establishment of a professional military, it lost those who had joined to avoid conscription into the Army. The transition to the AVF thus led to shortages for many land jobs (e.g. jobs located overseas, equipment maintenance, aircraft ground crews, intelligence, and communications) and on non-combat aircrafts and ships. Since the late 1970s, women were thus increasingly integrated to fill these positions. Despite resistance within the Navy, personnel needs triumphed over ideological considerations, and women were first sent to sea in 1978 (Iskra 2007: 204ff.). However, they were restricted from combat vessels until the early 1990s because these jobs were in higher demand (Brown 2006: 16ff.). These restrictions also fell with the new legislation. Though parts of the Navy publicly spoke out against integration, their chief of staff had explicitly asked Congress for legal reforms to grant more flexibility in assignments and deployments (Iskra 2007: 210).

For most of the past decades, the Navy's female participation rates were only slightly lower than in the Army and at times even higher. This reflects its large support structure and relatively high proportion of specialized jobs. Women's demand for Navy jobs is also high because qualifications acquired there are easily transferred to civilian labor markets (Harrel and Miller 1997: 24). The Navy was most affected by the 1990s legislation because more than half of the newly opened positions were on its combat vessels (Armor 1996: 14). It also opened combat aircraft to women. From this point on, 91.2 percent of positions were open to women. Limitations resulted from lack of accommodation on ships (Harrell/Miller 1997: 11) and exclusion from direct ground combat, inhibiting admission to the Navy SEALS. The new legislation strongly raised representation among enlisted personnel from 14 percent in 1992 to 20 percent in 1995 (Armor 1996: 14f.). At the same time, the Navy was hit hard by budget cutbacks after the

Persian Gulf War, in which it had played only a marginal role. Already during the Cold War, it had been considered oversized. Now, the number of ships was reduced and the aviation program was cut in favor of the Air Force (Gabbert 2007: 53). Within the institution, competition between seamen and pilots who had gained status in the course of modernization processes was increasing. Intensified competitiveness in the context of downsizing and restructuring coincided with increased women's integration. The conjunction of these processes of change provided the context for the sexual harassment and abuse of female Navy members during the Tailhook Convention in 1991. It also explains renewed restrictions on women's recruitment, which reduced their ratio among enlisted personnel to 16 percent in 1996 (Armor 1996: 14f.).

The Air Force has the longest experience with women's integration though it is the youngest service. Only here were women integrated from the onset in 1947. The Air Force is the technologically most advanced service with the largest support structure and strong demand for qualified personnel even in combat positions. It therefore has the highest percentage of female personnel. Simultaneously, it attracts enough qualified men and rarely has to actively recruit. While other services sometimes have to chose between better qualified women and less qualified men, the Air Force can demand higher qualification standards from men without fearing shortages. Hence, women were most rigorously kept from its core mission, aviation (ibid.: 25ff.). Since the Air Force had been least affected by combat exclusion laws, it could accommodate the changes of the 1990s relatively easily. Technical adaptations were minimal, since equipment was already adjusted to men who did not conform to the average height and weight of American men. Standards and organizational procedures for selecting qualified women were also already in place (Asch *et al.* 2001: 17). The increase in female enlisted service members was less pronounced, with 22 percent before and 24 percent after restrictions fell (Armor 1996: 14). Budget cutbacks, however, complicated the situation. Cockpit-positions were affected by downsizing after the Cold War, and competition for these was fierce. Already in the early 1990s, the Air Force had more qualified pilots than cockpits to fill (Lancaster 1993). After other services had demanded that the Air Force restrict women to decrease its competitive advantages in recruiting, they were excluded from some positions. Contrary to other services, these closed positions were not crucial to a career in the Air Force (Asch *et al.* 2001: 15).

The Marine Corps has always been the most hesitant in regard to gender integration. Formally, the Marines are part of the Navy, but are often perceived as a force in their own right because they have a representative in the Joint Chiefs of Staff and their own military academy. The Navy assumes most of their supply and support tasks, which explains the Marines' high proportion of combat troops, especially ground combat, and of jobs for less qualified personnel. A large contingent of jobs is thus closed to women by law. Especially during peacetime, demand for female labor is extremely low. Recruitment increases only during wartime to free men for combat jobs (Harrell and Miller 1997: 32ff.), leading to the lowest female representation within any service. Because the Marines were less affected by modernization processes, this representation remained relatively stable at a low level between 4 percent and 6 percent from the late 1970s until today (Armor 1996: 15). The lack of a nurse corps leads to the lowest rate of female officers, because all nurses are officers (Stiehm 1996: 67). The transitions of the early 1990s did not change this situation much. Due to the small and elitist leadership structure and the high ratio of ground combat troops, the lack of specialist non-combatants that prompted other services to increasingly recruit women did not apply to the Marines. In addition to legal impediments—only 62 percent of positions are open to women—assignment and recruitment policies also account for low representation. The lifting of the "risk rule" opened 48,000 new positions (WREI n.d.), most of them on combat vessels. But the newly opened positions were only marginally filled with women (2 percent). One explanation was women's lower average scores on the technical qualification tests required for most of these positions. Furthermore, the Marines neither targeted women for recruitment and assignment to formerly closed positions, nor transferred them thereto (Asch *et al.* 2001: 26ff.).

State transformation and military privatization

Modernization of gender relations in the military and women's increased integration mirror transformations of the relationship between the state and the military. In its earlier stages, professionalization of warfare had fostered a specific connection between state, war, and masculinity. The further this process advanced, the more this relationship was loosened. Under the conditions of industrialized production and mechanized warfare, efficiency was raised by centralizing state control over military organization and conscripting men into nation-state militaries. Under the conditions of a service-economy and technological warfare, the military was turned into a labor market reigned by supply and demand. Conscripts became volunteers and the relationship between military institutions and their personnel changed from one defined as a temporary obligation to the state to a career (Segal and Segal 1983: 160). The exclusive connection between man and state, which the military had produced and strengthened, was thus weakened: service was no longer a (male) citizen's duty, but a profession. For reasons outlined above, this professionalization was accompanied by abolishment of conscription and opening up towards women, leading to a rationalization of gender ideologies. The relationship between state, military service, and masculinity became less rigid thanks to the volunteer force and subsequent women's integration. These developments questioned the status of the military as a male resource of power directly related to the state.

The privatization of military tasks further dissolves the specific relationship between state and men. Economic globalization, advanced technology and professionalism in warfare, and the crisis of the Western state represent the context for the boom of marketized security over the past decades. General tendencies towards privatization and denationalization of state responsibilities began in the 1970s, when economic growth was severely curtailed and domestic industry began to migrate to countries with lower wages and commodity costs. This migration increased pressure on the state, weakened its institutions, and introduced neo-liberal policies of deregulation (Prokop 2001: 381). From the mid-1990s, access to untapped markets, in terms of purchasing power and workforce, became a crucial economic asset and was thus supported through military interventions. The weakening of the state furthered market deregulation and the outsourcing of traditional state responsibilities to private companies, also in the military sector. Under these conditions, differentiation of military tasks was accompanied by increased employment of private military companies (PMCs) (Segal/Segal 2004: 4, 37). Market-supplied security flourished since the early 1990s (Chesterman 2007). Between 1994 and 2002 the Pentagon concluded 3,000 contracts with US companies worth 300 billion dollars (Avant and Sigelman 2009: 5).

Transformation of military gender ideologies

> At the end of the year [when the Naval Academy holds its graduation ceremony], the company with the highest military rating serves as the "color company," and one permitted to carry the colors in the ceremonial Color Parade held during graduation week before scores of invited guests and dignitaries. The midshipman who commands the color company invites his girlfriend, whom the Naval Academy flies in, dresses in splendor, and enters in the parade as the "color girl." ... Some critics muse about the day when a female midshipman happens to be commander of the color company. Will there then be a "color boy"? Will an African-American midshipman someday command the color company and invite his girlfriend to be the "color girl"?
>
> (Burke 1996: 207)

As outlined in the previous chapters, women have been gradually and selectively integrated into the US volunteer military since the 1970s. The present study shows how the evolving patterns of gender-specific labor division affect ideologies of masculinity and femininity. Previous research on this issue has mainly concentrated on constructions of military masculinity or has surveyed service members' attitudes towards women's integration. The results to date provide important evidence on the cultural dimensions of gender integration. This evidence supports the hypotheses of ideological diversification and adaptation to structural conditions. Despite their different research foci, many studies indicate that the dissolution of clear gender-specific boundaries in the military has led to a differentiation of military ideals of masculinity and femininity.

One undisputed result of gender and military research is that we can no longer speak of a single, monolithic concept of military masculinity. Diversified tasks are reflected in diversified images that correspond to status and position within the institution. Frank Barrett (1999) has shown for the US Navy that different occupational fields develop different masculine ideals. In his survey, pilots claimed hegemonic ideals such as aggression, technical competence, courage, and autonomy for themselves, while naval officers emphasized endurance of physical hardship and discipline as sources of their professional ethos. The growing group of support officers focused on rationality and responsibility for resources in their self-portrayals. They mostly depicted themselves as specialists, aspiring to a career in private economy, and conformed to neo-liberal values of a corporate masculinity. Cynthia Enloe (1988) has also described differential ideals for soldiers, officers, generals, or "defense intellectuals." Even popular culture produces depictions that reach from technological, rational masculinity to the sentimental portrayals of the soldier in the domestic sphere (Wiegman 1994: 173). Still, not all of these ideals are ascribed the same value. The higher the status und pay, the more a group is associated with traditional stereotypes of aggressive, fearless, and war-prone masculinity.

In the course of organizational and strategic modernization of warfare, aggressive and individualistic masculinity ideals have always been counter-balanced by the notion of conformity and discipline: "While the image of the manly warrior plays an ideological role in the military, with real consequences, this image coexists in complex ways with the requirements of organized warfare that prevail against the masculinist ideal" (Titunik 2008: 147). The ongoing convergence of military and civilian realms and differentiation of military occupations have further "civilized" masculinity ideals. Traditional gender stereotypes lost some of their relevance as argumentations for inclusions and exclusions, while individual performance gained importance: "The process of rationalization in society entails increasing emphasis on individual achievement and a de-emphasis on ascriptive characteristics" (Segal and Segal 1983: 164). At the same time, traditional concepts are retained to uphold remaining boundaries, such as women's exclusion from ground combat.

Increased fluidity between civilian and military labor markets has enhanced fluidity between the respective gender ideologies. This exchange goes both ways, not only civilizing military masculinity, but also militarizing civilian masculinity. Susan Jeffords (1989) observed the latter during the Reagan era, when popular culture compensated for the loss of social status of many (white) men during the 1970s by a remasculinization of gender images. Militarization of foreign policy and social change after the Vietnam War, which was interpreted as an attack on American masculinity and the traditional nuclear family, provided the context for this successful reinstallation of masculinist ideology (Niva 1998: 110ff.). Accordingly, the Reagan administration was able to construct Vietnam veterans as the victims of an "unmanly" civil society consisting of civil rights and women's movements that refused them their status as heroes. These beliefs were fostered by the fact that the social status of Vietnam veterans was not only discursively, but also materially inferior to that of veterans of the Korean and Second World War, who had experienced some upward social mobility due to the GI Bill (Segal and Segal 2004: 16). The narrative of demasculinization through the defeat in Vietnam was again successfully employed to mobilize for the Persian Gulf War.

Concepts of military femininity have attracted far less scientific scrutiny than their masculine counterparts. Research on the German Bundeswehr, however, provides informative evidence on how femininity ideologies adapt to the form and degree of integration. Ruth Seifert (1996) has shown that the more women are integrated in the regular troops, the more gender-neutral definitions of military professionalism become and the more women are accepted in non-combat positions. On the level of discourse and within personnel policy, combat and leadership represent the new ideological core of military masculinity.

Darlene Iskra's (2007) analysis of internal Navy debates provides important insights into the relations between gender ideologies and argumentations for and against integration. It shows that opponents and supporters both referred to military efficiency and readiness in debates. Opponents blamed women for decreasing troop cohesion and motivation of soldiers and their families. They accused women of being inexperienced, unmotivated, diverting male soldiers from their mission, unwilling to serve in all positions, and also unneeded. Some of these arguments remained a constant from the 1970s to the twenty-first century, such as the depiction of integration as a "social experiment," the necessity of protecting women against captivity and rape by the enemy, the danger of fraternization, and the negative attitudes of military wives. Advocates of integration, in turn, tried to show that women had positive effects on readiness, were motivated, disciplined, and available. Gender was argued an insufficient reason for exclusion. Additionally, supporters of an expanded role referred to civil rights and democratic values.

Despite these continuities, Iskra demonstrated that the argumentative contents and strategies varied quantitatively and qualitatively as they adapt to social and military conditions. Morality and traditional gender roles were the main opposing considerations during the late 1970s, while women's lack of physical abilities and the danger of double standards were more frequently emphasized during the 1990s. Traditional gender stereotypes remained influential, but they less often referred to the protection of women and family than to women's inability to assert themselves within the male military world. After these abilities were proven by the late 1990s, such prejudice could not be upheld. Hence, argumentative strategies of opponents refocused on sexual relationships between service members, sexual abuse, false accusations of sexual harassment, and fear of exaggerated "political correctness." Supporters of integration and equality held that only the abolishment of institutional discrimination could make military women equal members of the armed forces. Iskra's research material consists of letters to the editor in Navy journals, but the public discourse on gender integration features very similar content and a similar relationship between pragmatic and value-oriented argumentation. The shift from "technical" argumentations to concerns about sexual morals during the 1990s was also observable in the examined media debates.

Though "public opinion" is often introduced to argue both for and against women's integration, there are only a few actual analyses of public debate and the arguments used within it. Processes of military gender construction within general society are thus relatively under-researched. Polls suggest that the general population is slightly more conservative than the military when it comes to issues of gender integration. In a 2001 survey, 28.2 percent of Americans agreed with the statement: "The military should remain basically masculine, dominated by male values and characteristics," while only 17.4 percent of Pentagon civilians and 14.6 percent of military leadership were of this opinion (Feaver/Kohn 2001: 377). An analysis of media reporting on military gender issues (Hanson 2002) revealed, on the other hand, that the media generally supports equality measures and has helped military women's agendas by pressuring political and military leadership. This positive stance, however, came with a price: it promoted stereotypes of military women as "damsels in distress"—a label that is particularly harmful to the image of service members. Media representatives presented themselves as protectors of these women and focused on "sex scandals" with women in the role of the victim, while neglecting "success stories" and informative reporting. Here, too, a "sexualization" of the debate is evident.

These research results enable drawing certain conclusions on ideologies of femininity within the military and general society. They also help reconstruct the discursive context of media debates. No systematic study of changes in constructions of femininity in relation to social and military structural change has yet been put forward. The following chapters supplement what is already known on military gender ideologies and show that diversified military masculinity ideals are accompanied by diversified femininity ideals. The "damsel in distress" is complemented by the professional soldier, the patriotic heroine, but also the sexualized destroyer of military institutions and values. The relative importance of each stereotype is defined by social, military, and political conditions and power relations between different interest groups. These conditions are evaluated for the different phases of the investigation period to highlight their impact on the ideological level and reconstruct the change of gender ideologies in media debates.

4 Military gender ideologies in the media

After having established the historical contexts and developments as well as the major social, military, and political factors influencing gender integration, the next step is to analyze media discourses in order to reconstruct the transformation of gender ideologies from 1990 to 2005. Based on Critical Historical Discourse Analysis (CHDA) (Wodak 2001), media debates on military gender integration were examined in an exemplary case study of reporting in the US daily newspapers *The New York Times* (NYT) and *The Washington Post* (WP). Table 4.1 displays the distribution of articles on military women and their integration across genres, newspapers, and years of publication. This overview reveals three quantitative peaks in reporting on military gender issues in the examined time frame, each located in one of the three separately investigated phases (phase 1: 1990–1994; phase 2: 1995–1999; phase 3: 2000–2005). The most pronounced rise in articles occurred in the early 1990s, when a large-scale military intervention prominently featured military women, and many bans on their assignment and deployment were lifted. The infamous "Tailhook scandal" also falls into this time period. The second peak was a rather isolated one in 1997, when many "sex scandals" within the military came to light and/or were negotiated in court. The last quantitative height in reporting coincides with the invasion of Iraq in the course of the "War on Terror." The structural reasons for these tendencies and the specific topics that caused these peaks are discussed in more detail when the different phases of the investigated period are scrutinized.

The first step: contents of media discourses

The first step in CHDA is to identify the specific contents of a particular discourse, in the present case the media discourse on military gender integration. Based on the analyzed articles, two main categories of statements could be defined: first, depictions of military women, their characteristics, and abilities (or lack thereof) and, second, depictions of integration processes. While the first were mostly uttered in a descriptive, "neutral" manner in features and reportages, the second more often took the linguistic structure of argumentation, often within op-ed articles and commentaries. In many cases, the two groups were intertwined, as attributes of (military) women were often used to argue for or against integration,

Table 4.1 Distribution of articles across newspapers, genres, and time

	The New York Times				The Washington Post				Total
	Reports	Features	Editorials	Total	Reports	Features	Editorials	Total	
1990	2	0	0	2	1	1	3	5	7
1991	4	4	2	10	3	0	4	7	17
1992	3	0	3	6	2	3	1	6	12
1993	3	1	2	6	2	0	2	4	10
1994	2	0	0	2	1	0	0	1	3
1995	0	0	0	0	0	0	0	0	0
1996	1	1	0	2	0	0	0	0	2
1997	4	2	2	8	4	0	1	5	13
1998	0	0	0	0	0	0	1	1	1
1999	1	0	0	1	0	0	0	0	1
2000	0	0	0	0	1	0	0	1	1
2001	0	0	0	0	0	0	2	2	2
2002	0	0	0	0	0	1	0	1	1
2003	1	1	2	4	0	1	4	5	9
2004	0	0	0	0	0	3	1	4	4
2005	1	2	1	4	4	3	2	9	13
Total	22	11	12	45	18	12	21	51	96

and the nature of integration was argued as (in)compatible with alleged characteristics of (military) women. A separate treatment of these groups highlights how ideological conceptions are incorporated within argumentation strategies. The study includes quantitative and qualitative elements. It does not aim at uncovering the strategic intention behind every single statement, but at identifying trends in the relative representation of different groups of statements across different groups of actors over a certain period of time.

The analysis began by elaborating on what was written in the investigated media about military women and their integration. This established the contents of discourse. Statements with multiple contents were classified under more than one category. Statement groups were divided into positive and negative categories, which serve descriptive purposes and implies no value judgment. Some categories appeared in a negative and a positive version, thus possessing the structure of argument/counter-argument. Hence, many categories stood in a relationship of reciprocity to each other. The following categories of statements were identified:

Positive statements on military women:

- Military women are courageous and fierce
- Military women are patriotic and heroic
- Military women are professional and competent
- Military women are able to endure hardship
- Military women are emancipated and progressive
- Military women are reliable comrades
- Motherhood and military service are compatible.

- Military women are qualified for leadership
- Military women already serve in combat positions
- Military women want to serve in combat positions.

Positive statements on gender integration:

- Integration contributes to military effectiveness
- Integration helps overcome out-dated values
- Integration is consistent with the performance principle
- Integration is supported by the public
- Integration enhances gender equality
- Integration is patriotic and symbolizes US progressiveness
- Protection of women is not a valid argument against integration
- War neutralizes gender differences
- Gender integration parallels racial integration
- Exclusion fosters sexual abuse.

Negative statements on military women:

- Military women are mentally unfit
- Military women are physically unfit
- Motherhood is incompatible with military service
- Military women do not want to serve in combat positions
- Male soldiers are against military women
- Military women do not possess a warrior ethos
- Military women cannot assert themselves in the male world of the military
- Military service masculinizes women
- Military women are cruel.

Negative statements on gender integration:

- Integration hinders military effectiveness
- Integration is against US values
- Integration is a concession to "political correctness"
- The public is against integration
- Women need to be protected
- Military service contradicts feminist values
- Integration causes sexual abuse
- Gender integration is not comparable to racial integration.

Before exploring the distribution of these statements across different phases of the examined time period in depth and contextualizing the media content within social, military, and political conditions, each category will be briefly elaborated to highlight variations in contents and intersections with other categories. Each will be illustrated by examples from the analyzed articles. The strategic moment in statements can be identified only in relation to its context: by ascribing it to a group of actors and locating these actors and their interests within processes of social and military change. This will be the subsequent step in the discourse analysis.

Positive statements on military women

Military women are courageous and fierce

Among the most frequent statements were portrayals of military women as fearless fighters, who were ambitious and ready for combat. During the intervention in the Persian Gulf, pilot and POW Rhonda Cornum was particularly often shown as ballsy and strong (Allen 1992, WP: f.01; Gellman 1992, WP: a.03; Sciolino 1992, NYT: A1). Even the danger of being raped did not deter her and others from their mission as soldiers:

> Culler, who is from Fayetteville, N.C., said the thought of being captured doesn't deter her. "That comes with the territory," she said. "I know the risks involved."
>
> (Vobejda and Health 1993, WP: A.06)

Female soldiers were shown as tough and ready for combat (Janovsky 1997, NYT: A10; Rayner 1997, NYT: 6/25). They were looking forward to challenges and served as integral members of the services in dangerous positions (Scott Tyson 2005a, WP: A.08; Scott Tyson 2005e, WP; A.01; Marcus 2005, WP: A.17; Cave 2005, NYT: A1):

> "Bravery," she said, "is not gender-specific." When men in Iraq try to tell her to stay on base, she pushes to join them in the field. "My role is to patch some-one up and get them out of trouble," she said. "I'll do it wherever I need to."
>
> (Cave 2005, NYT: A1)

Military women are patriotic and heroic

These statements featured female soldiers willing to die for their country and risk their lives, despite discrimination against them in the services (Moore 1990b, WP: a.01; Marano 1990, WP: b.01; Scott Tyson 2005b, WP: A.01):

> Sergeant Treloar is a walking, talking Army recruitment poster, the sort of soldier who makes it plain that she is proud to put her life on the line for "the American way of life."
>
> (Shenon 1991, NYT: 116)

Patriotism was claimed as a motivation for military service for women, too (Editorial 1991, NYT: A12), as they were equally striving to participate in the defense of the US constitution and its values (Myers 2003, NYT: A16). These values were then directly associated with gender equality measures in the military:

> "That is what my loyalty is to," she says, to the Constitution of the United States. "And my hope would be that they will say about this [gender equality] policy, "Here, it's changing." And I will say, "God Bless America."
>
> (Gerhart 2002, WP: C.01)

Features described how military women were honored as heroes by their families and home town communities, just like their male colleagues (Gellman 1992, WP. a.03; Sullivan 1991, NYT: B1). During the Iraq intervention, women appeared as protectors of the Iraqi civilian population, but also of their families and their fatherland (Loeb 2003, WP: D.01). They saved male soldiers (Scott Tyson 2005b, WP: A.01; Gerhart 2001, WP: C.01) and were awarded medals for valor (Scott Tyson 2005e, WP: A.01; Fainaru 2005, WP: A.01).

Military women are professional and competent

Professionalism and competence were the most frequently mentioned positive characteristics of military women, who were often portrayed as competitive, dutiful, and rational (Sciolino 1990, NYT: A1; Priest 1991a, WP: a.10; Editorial 1993, WP: a.20). They wanted to be treated as soldiers and not be spared any hardship (Moore 1990b, WP: a.01; Schmitt 1994b, NYT). High levels of qualification, discipline, work ethic, and expertise were often ascribed to military women, but sometimes also associated with a desirable level of obedience that men lacked (Lawrence 1991, WP: c.07). These characteristics were also cited as evidence that women could outperform men in some areas (Moskos 1998, WP: C.01):

> [W]omen have an educational edge, "much less of a discipline problem, lose less time even with pregnancy. Men have established patterns of alcohol and discipline problems."
>
> (Ret. Army Cpt., in: Mann 1992, WP: d.23)

Past performances of women were cited as the grounds for providing them with new opportunities:

> [The Pentagon report states that women] were killed, injured and captured in the war, military women involved were "enormously capable and professional," and that they "performed their missions with distinction."
>
> (Cushman 1993a, NYT: A1)

Military women are able to endure hardship

While such statements appeared rather rarely in the analyzed reporting, some articles featured military women's perseverance to implicitly or explicitly counter depictions of a lack of physical and psychological capabilities. Military women were thus shown as enduring the hardships of military life effortlessly (Sciolino 1990, NYT: A1):

> "We get paid the same. We have an equal opportunity to die for our country. You live with the possibility of somebody dropping a bomb on you or some terrorist blowing you up. But you do what you have to do out here."
>
> (Moore 1990b, WP: a.01)

These depictions often pointed out the performance of women in physically challenging civilian jobs, such as the police or the fire brigade (Editorial 1990, WP: a.20). Women were portrayed as stable, reliable, and resilient (Mann 1992, WP: d.23; Ricks 2000, WP: A.03; Fears 2004, WP: A.01), despite discrimination against them (Macur 2005, NYT). They did not want any kind of protection or privilege (Scott Tyson 2005b, WP: A.01) and were able to stay calm, even in combat situations (Fainaru 2005, WP: A.01):

> "Before this war, people only imagined how women would react in combat roles and thought that they couldn't handle it. But for the first time women are shooting back and doing heavy lifting in a real war. The bullets are real, so are the roadside bombs and the blood. Now we see that women are bonding with the men and not going to pieces."
>
> (Lory Manning, ret. Navy Capt., Women's Research and Education Institute, in: Macur 2005, NYT)

Military women are emancipated and progressive

These attributes mostly came up when female soldiers were portrayed as contradicting Muslim culture in the Arab countries, in which they were stationed (Moore 1990b, WP: a.01):

> Americans have come to see this emancipation of women as a freedom worth fighting for. The way we treat women makes us different from the Taliban, better than terrorists.
>
> (Goodmann 2001, WP: A25)

American military women were shown as independent and self-confident, as they asserted themselves against Muslim misogyny, their male colleagues, military leadership, and even their own families (Shenon 1991, NYT: 116; Moore 1990a, WP: d.01; Gerhart 2002, WP: C.01; Scott Tyson 2005b, WP: A.01). They thought unconventionally and were loyal to each other (Sciolino 1992, NYT: A1; Gellman 1992, WP: a.03; Allen 1992, WP: f.01). They decided and acted independently and demanded their right to be treated as a soldier (Wilgoren 2003, NYT: B1; Fears 2004, WP: A.01; Fainaru 2005, WP: A.01). These characteristics made them pioneers and role models for future generations:

"The women of the future can look up to them, not because they died but because they served," said Cpl. Johnny Francisco, 21, a marine administrator.
(Cave 2005, NYT: A1)

In some of these statements, military service itself was depicted as emancipating because it strengthened self-confidence and provided opportunities missing in other institutions (Egan 1996, NYT: A14).

Military women are reliable comrades

Infrequently, but nevertheless, some articles featured women who cared about the wellbeing of their units more than about their own careers and worked together well with their comrades (Sciolino 1990, NYT: A1; Priest 1991b, WP: a.01; Rohter 1993, NYT: A1). Their male colleagues respected them for their stamina and performance (Wilgoren 2003, NYT: B1):

"I know the women are in a very difficult situation, but I give them credit for toughing it out. They have a very important job here."
(Male Lt. Col., Commander, in: Macur 2005, NYT)

These depictions are particularly relevant in the debate on integration, since a main argument of opponents has always been the destructive impact that women allegedly had on unit cohesion and their lack of ability to save and protect their comrades. To counter these arguments, it was claimed that shared combat experience welded men and women together and neutralized gender differences (Fainaru 2005, WP: A.01). Cohesion was not endangered by integration, but by inequality and discrimination. Additionally, women were well able to pull wounded comrades from the battlefield or secure their survival in other ways:

Far from shrinking from the fight, women in Iraq are winning medals for valor under fire. ... As her Humvee began to roll over, Hodges reached over and grabbed the legs of Pfc. Gregory Burchett, who was manning a .50-caliber machine gun. She pulled him down from the hatch and into the vehicle just before it flipped, saving him from being crushed.
(Scott Tyson 2005b, WP: A.01)

In some instances, these female saviors were associated with traditionally female characteristics such as motherliness and readiness to sacrifice.

Motherhood and military service are compatible

The debate on the compatibility of motherhood (not fatherhood) and military service was a main aspect of the overall debate on gender integration. Opponents frequently referred to the seeming contradiction between the responsibilities of a mother and the role of a soldier. Some statements nevertheless spoke up for mothers in military service and portrayed motherhood and child-care as resolvable organizational problems (Sciolino 1990, NYT: A1; Editorial 1991, NYT: A12; Sciolino 1992, NYT: A1; Vobejda/Health 1993, WP: A.06). Accordingly, it was possible to be a dedicated service member and a "normal" wife and mother at the same time (Allen 1992, WP: f.01). Exceptional rules for mothers were seen as a setback in the struggle for equality (Priest 1991a, WP: a.10). The voluntariness of military service was related to the feminist catch-word of "choice":

> "I would be very nervous about saying mothers can't serve. These mothers are volunteers. I don't see why a mother's choice should be any more restricted than a father's choice should be."
>
> (Economist and senior fellow at the Brookings Institution, in: Priest 1991a, WP: a.10)

Some statements argued that both spouses possessed equal rights to defend their country and that women were supported in their decisions and given credit for them by their husbands and children:

> Her husband, Atilano, is taking care of their children, ages 12, 10, 7 and 4. ... "It was my turn to serve the country and protect our children," says Sanchez. "They're worried. I know they're worried. My 4-year-old, she doesn't understand what is going on. But my 12-year-old understands everything that's going on. He knows I'm strong, taking care of myself."
>
> (Loeb 2003, WP: D.01)

Military women are qualified for leadership

Depictions of women as capable, respected, and reliable military leaders were particularly infrequent throughout the investigated period. Only very few statements featured women as responsible authoritative figures who were in command of men (Egan 1996, NYT: A14; Rohter 1993, NYT: A1; Embser-Herbert 2004, WP: B.01):

> Julia Mejia, with blue eyes and long hair tucked beneath a baseball cap, is the first woman in the Army to teach air assault. But for the soldiers on the tower, mostly male, shivering in the wind and driving rain, she represents not a nurturing feminine ideal but competence, the reassuring and not always kindly voice of command. She's the authority figure who will coax and cajole them through this. Bluntly put, she's power.
>
> (Rayner 1997, NYT: 6/25)

Military women already serve in combat positions

Some statements claimed that women were already serving in combat positions, but were still not recognized as full members of the military. Women were fulfilling their duty under dangerous conditions and deserved the lifting of discriminatory laws (Nordheimer 1991, NYT: 11; Shenon 1991, NYT: 116):

> [T]housands of other brave and capable women risked their lives for their country despite laws and policies intended to exclude them from combat. Ironically, the laws in practice exclude women only from equal opportunity— while leaving them fully in harm's way during wartime. Nothing could more properly honor the women who died than for Congress and the Pentagon to put an end to these discriminatory laws and practices.
>
> (Marano 1990, WP: b.01)

Since women were sacrificing for their country in the same way men did, they claimed the same kind of respect and support. The danger of demoralizing them through discriminatory rules and practices was used as an argument for lifting bans (Shanker 2005, NYT: A20; Editorial 2005, NYT: A24; Cave 2005, NYT: A1; Macur 2005, NYT). Women's daily confrontations with combat were set against politicians' unawareness of the realities of war (Scott Tyson 2005b, WP: A.01):

> "You can't tell me I'm not being shot at. You can't tell me I can't handle combat," said Provancha, who has nearly been hit by road bombs, rockets and the chow hall suicide bombing that killed 22 in December. "That was pretty frickin" direct fire if you ask me," she said, holding up a piece of shrapnel.
>
> (Fainaru 2005, WP: A.01)

Military women want to serve in combat positions

On both sides of the debate, the wishes of military women were used as a relevant argument to support their claims. Statements supportive of more equality featured women who were eager to prove themselves in combat and convince through their performances (Moore 1990b, WP: a.01; Sciolino 1990, NYT: A1; Mann 1991, WP: d.03; Editorial 1992a, NYT: A18; Sciolino 1992, NYT: A1; Editorial 2005, NYT: A24; Scott Tyson 2005b, WP: A.01):

> Maj. Christine Prewitt, an Air Force pilot, said she strongly supported relaxing the current restrictions so she would be allowed to fly fighter jets and other warplanes. "Basically, you have to go out and prove yourself," she said. "After that it doesn't seem to matter you're a woman."
>
> (Schmitt 1991b, NYT: A16)

After the legal changes of the early 1990s, women were shown as celebrating the lifting of bans, as they had finally achieved justice and could now pursue their professional goals (Vobejda and Health 1993, WP: A.06; Rohter 1993, NYT: A1):

> Air Force Lt. Col. Kelly Hamilton, who flew tankers in the Gulf war and now is stationed in Hawaii, said she reacted with "absolute joy" when she heard

the news. "I've been flying now for 15 years, and this is something I'd looked forward to for a long time," she said in a telephone interview.

(Lancaster 1993, WP: A.01)

Positive statements on military gender integration

Integration contributes to military effectiveness

Military effectiveness has been the most prominently featured argument on both sides of the debate. Pro-integration arguments claimed that women's exclusion would harm military efficiency more than the excluded women (Sciolino 1990, NYT: A1; Editorial 1992b, NYT: 118; National Desk 1993, NYT: A30). Most of these statements referred to the quality of personnel, which could only be upheld by integrating women. Integration was depicted as pragmatic and rational, exclusion as irrational and counter-productive (Marano 1990, WP: b.01; Lawrence 1991, WP: c.07; Tyler May 1991, NYT: A21; Schmitt 1994a, NYT: A22). Discrimination would demoralize women and thereby endanger the war effort (Shanker 2005, NYT: A20; WP76 Scott Tyson 2005a, WP: A.08; Scott Tyson 2005c, WP: A.05):

> Right now, with a war raging, female soldiers vital to the effort need no demoralizing intrusion into the gender issue by impulsive lawmakers ... . Women have volunteered for the full range of opportunity and risk implicit in their military careers. They are proving their valor in Iraq and need no demeaning protections from Congress.
>
> (Editorial 2005, NYT: A24)

Gender equality and military needs were thus constructed as compatible (Nordheimer 1991, NYT: 11). Different lines of argumentation can be identified in this regard: One argued that integration was not a "gender issue" at all and that equality was only a side-effect of raising effectiveness. Others highlighted the interplay between equal opportunity and military benefits (Schmitt 1996, NYT: 114; Editorial 1997, WP: A.22). All arguments, however, implied that women should only be integrated to the extent to which it served military needs and national security:

> [This] order gives America's military women what they deserve: a fair chance to go as far as their talents will take them. America, too, is getting what it deserves: armed services in which competence matters more than gender.
>
> (Editorial 1993, WP: a.20)

Military efficiency of integration was also related to the trend towards peace-keeping operations: while "female" characteristics were a disadvantage in combat, they could be utilized in new forms of conflict that required cultural sensitivity, particularly when dealing with the civilian population (Moskos 1998, WP: C.01;

Macur 2005, NYT; Editorial 2005b, WP: A16). The misogynist values of the enemy were also to be utilized for military objectives (Kristof 2003, NYT: A31). Additionally, US military women were supposed to serve as advertisers of American values and win over the civilian population of the enemy:

> First, particularly in the Muslim world, notions of chivalry make even the most bloodthirsty fighters squeamish about shooting female soldiers or blowing them up at checkpoints. ... Let's let foreign chauvinism work for us. Second, wars these days are less for territory than for hearts and minds, and coed military units appear less menacing. ... Moreover, one of the reasons we go to war is to uphold values—like equality for all. We transmit that message every time our troops encounter foreigners, particularly when our soldiers have flowers in their helmets and names like Claire.
>
> (Wilgoren 2003, NYT: B1)

Integration helps overcome out-dated values

This kind of argumentation criticized women's exclusion as anachronistic (Moore 1990b, WP: a.01; Tyler May 1991, NYT: A21; Nordhcimcr 1991, NYT: 11) and accused military policy as being governed by archaic and uncivilized masculinism (Schmitt 1991c, NYT: A1):

> "In view of their distinguished service, blanket denial of combat roles to women strikes many people as outdated and unfair."
>
> (Republican Senator of Arizona John McCain,
> in: Schmitt 1991b, NYT: A16)

In many instances, the point of reference was not military effectiveness, but the necessary modernization of cultural values. The problem was seen in military culture that had to and could be changed (Vobejda/Health 1993, WP: A.06; National Desk 1993, NYT: A30). Traditional masculinist values were described as ridiculous and only upheld by "old men" (Priest 1997a, WP: a.02; Priest 1997c, WP: A.01):

> The Army's rule prohibiting women from working in direct support of combat units "was written for the old school, for men who thought women shouldn't be shot at," said Morgenthaler. "Do female MPs get as much credit as male infantry? Not today. I would like to think they would in the future."
>
> (Civil Affairs Reservist Lt. Col. Jill Morgenthaler,
> in: Priest 1997d, WP: A.01)

Integration is consistent with the performance principle

These statements constructed performance as the governing principle of political and military decision-making. As opposed to "effectiveness arguments," they focused on individual achievement rather than on women's merits as a group. Following this argumentation, a modern society was to select the best for the job, regardless of group affiliations such as gender. While this principle was already implemented in the civilian area, it needed to be established in the military as well (Marano 1990, WP: b.01). By doing so, all problems would be resolved automatically:

> Nevertheless, some combat-related assignments undoubtedly require the kind of physical strength most women don't have. Applicants for these positions should simply be tested, with the same standards applied to men and women. ... But in this day and age it's an insult and an injustice to be told you can't even apply for a job because yours is the weaker sex.
>
> (Editorial 1990, WP: a.20)

In these statements, individualism and performance led to equality and the overcoming of prejudice (Schmitt 1991a, NYT: 132; Nordheimer 1991, NYT: 11; Editorial 1991, NYT: A12; Gellman 1992, WP: a.03;Editorial 2003, NYT; Wilgoren 2003, NYT: B1):

> [I]f the goal in the military is to find the best fit between job requirements and individual abilities, then individuals should be selected for jobs on the basis of those abilities, not gender.
>
> (Sociologist, University of Maryland, in: Schmitt 1996, NYT: 114)

Integration is supported by the public

Very few statements named the public's positive attitudes towards integration as a relevant argument. Some argued that women were already doing dangerous jobs in the civilian realm and that the public was thus used to seeing women in these positions. To counter the "body-bag argument" which held that the public was unwilling to accept women being killed in a war, some claimed that the public was not perceiving killed female soldiers as a scandal, but honored them as heroines. The life of a woman was not to be valued more than the life of a man (Fears 2004, WP: A.01; Applebaum 2003, WP: A.17):

> The public understands that people who serve in the military can be killed, regardless of their gender. Thus, the public is taking the deaths of women in stride, and, rightfully, mourning for all the casualties of the Cole as sailors and heroes.
>
> (Female ret. Navy Capt., in: Ricks 2000, WP: A.03)

Integration enhances gender equality

Equality was an important issue for supporters of integration. Nonetheless, it was cited less often than effectiveness and performance. Supporters of equal opportunity highlighted discriminations against military women and the contradictions inherent in the current rules and regulations (Moore 1990b, WP: a.01). They claimed that combat exclusion did not protect women from danger, but kept them from promotion and career advancement (Editorial 1990, WP: a.20; Sciolino 1990, NYT: A1; Marano 1990, WP: b.01; Moore 1991, WP: a.01). Their status and their morale were thus weakened (Lancaster 1992, WP: a.03; Gellman 1992, WP: a.03):

> The current halfway house is unfair to women because as targets, they frequently are in combat, but are treated officially as though they are not. Not being officially allowed to hold combat positions prevents them from competing equally for promotion.
>
> (Rayner 1997, NYT: 6/25)

Equality in the services was also discussed as an important step towards full citizenship rights for women and enhanced status within society in general (Vobejda/Health 1993, WP: A.06).

Integration is patriotic and symbolizes US progressiveness

Besides depictions of patriotic military women, patriotism was also a frequent general argument for integration. The focus here was not on the patriotic attitudes of military women but on those who supported integration as an act of patriotism. Denying women equality was described as "un-American" and integration as a patriotic measure (Wilgoren 2003, NYT: B1):

> But to McSally, the directive, with its different instructions for men and women, "abandons our American values that we all raised our right hand to die for."
>
> (Air Force fighter pilot Martha McSally, in: Gerhart 2002, WP: C.01)

All patriots—male or female—should thus get a chance to fight for their country (Editorial 1990, WP: a.20). Additionally, true patriots would willingly risk their daughters' lives for the defense of the homeland (Gellman 1992, WP: a.03):

> My support of an expanded role for women in the Armed Forces is my final contribution. I believe we must fill our ranks with our best, regardless of gender.... In doing so I will proudly risk far more than other Commissioners—I risk my son and my daughter.
>
> (Commissioner Marine Brig. Gen. Thomas Draude,
> in: Editorial 1992b, NYT: 118)

Another important version of the patriotism argument referred to military women's roles as symbols of US progressiveness and diversity, in contrast to "suppressed"

Muslim women in backward Arab cultures (Reuters 1990, NYT: A17; Marano 1990, WP: b.01; Shenon 1991, NYT: 116; Reid 2003, WP: A19; Fainaru 2005, WP: A.01):

> Now US military women have not only entered the kingdom in large numbers, but have been granted freedoms that Saudi Arabian culture denies its women, including driving automobiles and use of government athletic facilities.
>
> (Moore 1990b, WP: a.01)

Women's military integration was presented as an American tradition, distinguishing the US from their Arab enemies (Wilgoren 2003, NYT: B1; Shanker 2005, NYT: A20; Scott Tyson 2005e, WP: A.01; Goodman 2001, WP: A.25; Gerhart 2002, WP: C.01; Kristof 2003, NYT: A31). Exclusion and discrimination contradicted the "freeing" of Muslim women as a war objective and endangered the war effort (Goodman 2001, WP: A.25; Shanker 2005, NYT: A20; Scott Tyson 2005a, WP: A.08; Scott Tyson 2005c, WP: A.05; Editorial 2005, NYT: A24).

Protection of women is not a valid argument against integration

The argument that women had to be excluded from certain military tasks for their own safety was countered by a number of statements which argued that women were only "protected" when it hindered their careers (Marano 1990, WP: b.01). Others claimed that, due to new forms of warfare, women in support units were equally endangered as combat troops and their alleged protection thus impossible and hypocritical (Ricks 2000, WP: A.03):

> "Who can take to the floor and say we must keep the combat-exclusion [laws] because this is how we keep women out of harm's way?" said Rep. Patricia Schroeder (D-Colo.), a long-time advocate of opening more jobs to women. "They saw how artificial all that was—the idea that you don't want women killed and you don't want women prisoners. We had some of those," she said.
>
> (Moore 1991, WP: a.01)

The hypocrisy of the protection argument was also highlighted by hinting at the problem of domestic violence and women in dangerous jobs in civilian life (Mann 1991, WP: d.03; Allen 1992, WP: f.01):

> Others argue that men should protect women, not the other way around. That chivalry might make some sense if it operated anywhere else in our society. But women are at risk in other occupations, where hazards to their safety abound. It is disingenuous to hear calls for their protection in battle when they are not even protected at home, where domestic abuse and violence against women are widespread.
>
> (Tyler May 1991, NYT: A21)

Since the possibility of being raped by the enemy constituted one of the most important argument of opponents, supporters argued that men could also be raped and that military women were more often harassed and abused by their fellow soldiers than by the enemy (Sciolino 1992, NYT: A1).

War neutralizes gender differences

In some statements, gender was depicted as an irrelevant category in warfare. Qualifications for and interest in military service were equally distributed across genders (Editorial 1990, WP: a.20; Gellman 1992, WP: a.03; Priest 1991b, WP: a.01) and troops developed a gender-neutral warrior ethos, which generated cohesion beyond gender borders. Additionally, technology rendered physical differences obsolete (Rohter 1993, NYT: A1). Recruits were standardized as gender-neutral soldiers (Janovsky 1997, NYT: A10; Rayner 1997, NYT: 6/25):

> "I see a soldier, a person," said Staff Sgt. William Eaker .... "She raised her right hand just as I did. ... Do I think she's any more or less qualified or more or less able to handle it because she's a female? No."
>
> (Wilgoren 2003, NYT: B1)

The military was constructed as a collective body in which all members were equally absorbed. War and death did not differentiate between the sexes, nor did heroism, courage, and performance (Editorial 2005, NYT: A24; Cave 2005, NYT: A1; Ricks 2000, WP: A.03; Myers 2003, NYT: A16):

> Capt. Todd Lindner, who commands the 617th Military Police Company, which includes Raven 42, said Hester and Pullen "shouldn't be held up as showpieces for why there should be women in combat. They should be held up as examples of why it's irrelevant."
>
> (Fainaru 2005, WP: A.01)

At times, this neutralization was also depicted as a loss of femininity that women also suffered from (Macur 2005, NYT).

Gender integration parallels racial integration

A few pro-arguments related gender integration to the civil rights movement and the integration of African-Americans and other minorities into the military. Women's participation was depicted as a logical step in a general process which provided more and more social groups with the opportunity to serve their country:

> We now have another group looking for the same chance to prove to the country their value, their talents, their dedication and their courage.
>
> (Marine Brig. Gen. Thomas V. Draude, in: Gellman 1992, WP: a.03)

Neither race nor gender should be relevant to recruitment (Schmitt 1996, NYT: 114 Schmitt 1992, NYT: 43). Note that comparisons with racial integration were also used as an argument against specific programs to enhance women's opportunities, since each "minority" had to adapt to the (male) military culture on its own (Priest 1997c, WP: A.01).

Exclusion fosters sexual abuse

Relating exclusion to sexual abuse was a common argument which countered statements that constructed the danger of sexual violence as a valid reason for exclusion (Schmitt 1992, NYT: 43; Gordon 1992, NYT: A10; Lancaster 1992, WP: a.03; Editorial 1993, WP: a.20). Consecutively, more integration and equality were identified as solutions to the problem (Rayner 1997, NYT: 6/25):

> All of my 20 years … in this business tells me that if you cannot share the equal risks and hazards in arduous duty, then you are not equal. And if the institution can discriminate against you, then it's not a big leap for … bigots to decide that "Well, I can harass you and I can get away with it."
> (Rosemary Mariner, former naval aviator, member of Joint Chiefs of Staff, in: Editorial 1992a, NYT: A18)

Negative statements on military women

Military women are mentally unfit

Among the most common negative depictions of military women were portrayals of them as fearful, child-like, and mentally weak (Moore 1990b, WP: a.01; Sciolino 1990, NYT: A1; McCarthy 1990, WP: f.02; Sullivan 1991, NYT: B1; Gonzales 1991, NYT: B4). Some also portrayed them as victims of feminists who instrumentalized them for their own political agendas (Quindlen 1992, NYT: A19). It was argued that women were unable to handle the rough military lifestyle (Editorial 1993, WP: a.20) and that their psychological instability made them unfit for service:

> The people who should be booted out of the service are the female officers who complained. If a grown woman can't handle some friendly drunks in a public place, then she's hardly qualified to command men in the much more serious and stressful environment of war.
> (Charley Reese in the Orlando Sentinel on Tailhook, in: Lancaster 1992, WP: a.03)

In such depictions, military women were in need of protection (Fears 2004, WP: A.01), naive, and unaware of what they had signed up for. In reality, they longed for a traditional life as a wife and mother (Wilgoren 2003, NYT: B1; Macur 2005, NYT). In many reports from the front, femininity was contrasted with the hardships of war. On the surface, the featured women seemed courageous, but at second glance their true identities as "typical girls" came through: they wore nail polish underneath their combat boots and were feeling empathically towards the enemy (Myers 2003, NYT: A16; Sheridan 2003, WP: A.01; Loeb 2003, WP: D.01). Even if they were at times able to act heroically, they couldn't cope with their own violence (Fainaru 2005, WP: A.01). Male soldiers were not portrayed as their comrades, but as their protective "older brothers":

> It was her first raid of an Iraqi home, and Pvt. Safiya Boothe, 21, had no idea what to expect. Tucking herself behind a group of men from her Army unit, her soft features and wispy body hidden by full battle gear, she walked through the front door, trying to be as anonymous as possible. When no shots were fired, she exhaled.
>
> (Macur 2005, NYT)

Military women are physically unfit

Carol Cohn (2000) has argued that reference to physical fitness plays an important role in integration debates: it allows military men to express "feelings of rage and loss about the way their institution has changed (or, for younger men, the ways it is different from the image that they grew up with)" (ibid.: 147). By doing so, male privileges can be defended against competition from female workforce in modernization processes in "a socially and institutionally acceptable way" (ibid.: 133). The analyzed material also frequently included depictions of women as flimsy and unfit for military requirements (Gellman 1992, WP: a.03; Editorial 1992, WP: a.21; Rohter 1993, NYT: A1), though prejudice pertaining to psychological weakness was even more common. The claim was that women were favored and thus undermined performance standards (Moore 1990b, WP: a.01; Schmitt 1994a, NYT: A22). Since modern warfare still required physical strength, "natural differences" had to be recognized (Moskos 1998, WP: C.01). Physical unfitness was also used to construct women as unreliable comrades (Hart Sinnreich 2001, WP: B.07; Wilgoren 2003, NYT: B1):

> But her husband, Lemoyne Sanders, 31, who spent four years in the Navy, said that behind sandbags or in an urban firefight, he would rather have a male soldier next to him than a woman. "You'll never get a woman to be as physically strong as a man," he said, adding: "Women get pregnant. It's just different."
>
> (Cave 2005, NYT: A1)

Motherhood is incompatible with military service

Depictions of military women as irresponsible, unhappy, or overstrained mothers were the most frequent negative statements about them. The traditional roles of women as natural caretakers and men as protectors of the family were considered the strongest argument against integration. In these statements, mothers and children were equally suffering when they were separated. Leaving children behind (or with their fathers) was considered unnatural behavior for a woman (Moore 1990b, WP: a.01; Mann 1991, WP: d.03; Becker 1999, NYT: A1; Nordheimer 1991, NYT: 11). Men who allowed for this to happen were accused of being unmanly:

> If a woman has a baby, she is completely responsible for the child. It's an embarrassment to the men of this country to send women to fight Iraqi President Saddam Hussein. They should show their manhood. The military should make a judgment that mothers are just like men with disabilities.
> (Phyllis Schlafly, Eagle Forum, in: Priest 1991a, WP: a.10)

Separating mothers and children was not only considered tragic for the families, but for society as a whole (Quinn 1991, WP: c.01). It was thus in the general public interest to treat mothers differently than fathers (Mann 1991, WP: d.03). Besides social consequences, mothers were also unable to do their jobs and take responsibility (Gordon 1992, NYT: A10; Gutman 1997, NYT: A31):

> Senior women officers who are mothers are strained beyond the limits. Whether it is genetic or cultural, women are more bonded to their children than men.
> (Charles Moskos, military sociologist at Northwestern University, in: Becker 1999, NYT: A1)

Women should be willing to waive their careers for their children and welcome the protection that exclusionary laws offered (Applebaum 2003, WP: A.17). All women were thus treated as potential mothers (Britt 2004, WP: B.01).

Military women do not want to serve in combat positions

These statements referred to the alleged wishes of "ordinary" military women who did not want to take part in the "male" job of combat (Schmitt 1991b, NYT: A16):

> "We like to do our part, but we don't want to go up front. That's a male's job. We don't want to go up there and get killed," she said.
> (Female Army Sgt., in: Moore 1991, WP: a.01)

Women officers were portrayed as selfish careerists who would sacrifice the lives of enlisted women for their own sake. The average military woman did not join the military because of career purposes and would thus not benefit from the lifting of bans (Nordheimer 1991, NYT: 11; Chavez 1993, WP: C3; Kreahling 1997, NYT: 13LI8). These women were counting on the protection offered by their male colleagues and the politicians in charge (Wilgoren 2003, NYT: B1; Macur 2005, NYT).

Male soldiers are against military women

Some articles featured military men who were against women's participation in combat because they saw themselves in the role of protectors and were "naturally" feeling at unease when women were present among the troops (Moore 1990b, WP: a.01):

> "I worried about her all the time," he said, "and being a POW and going through the torture, the pain, you shouldn't also have to worry about what's happening to the female soldier all the time."
>
> (Male Army Specialist, in: Sciolino 1992, NYT: A1)

Men were often shown as the victims of integration measures that put them under pressure and demasculinized them. They doubted women's abilities and didn't accept them, which was argued as the main reason for sexual violence against women (Cave 2005, NYT: A1; Macur 2005, NYT; Priest 1997c, WP: A.01; Baker 1997, NYT: 119). Male service members' feelings and concerns were to be considered in military decision-making (Schmitt 1992, NYT: 43; Rohter 1993, NYT: A1):

> The biggest unknown, though, is what the soldiers who will be most affected by the proposed changes think. The ones I interviewed, from buck privates to generals, raised detailed concerns that no one in Washington seems to be publicly discussing. And the closer one gets to the soldiers who will do the bleeding and dying, the more concerns they raise. Our country's leaders have a high moral responsibility to talk to these soldiers, to hear them out and to consider their views carefully.
>
> (Hackworth 1991, WP. a.25)

Military women do not possess a warrior ethos

These statements represent negative interpretations of women's professionalism. Their participation was delegitimized by portraying them as pragmatic and only interested in their careers, while men joined the military solely out of idealistic reasons. Women were thus diverging from military ideals:

> Many, like Dawn Lovingood, see the military as a good career move but have little appetite for the blood-and-guts aspects.
>
> (Rayner 1997, NYT: 6/25)

Additionally, military women were accused of taking advantage of their male colleagues, who did the "real work" and of taking public recognition away from them (Gutman 1997, NYT: A31; Cave 2005, NYT: A1; Macur 2005, NYT). In some instances, they were even said to destroy male soldiers' families and careers by wrongly accusing them of sexual misconduct (Brooke 1997, NYT: A10).

*Military women cannot assert themselves in the
male world of the military*

Statements depicting women as strangers in the military world were an ambivalent
category. They can be interpreted as criticism of discrimination, but also as
delegitimization of integration. Some articles portrayed the military as a male
bond in which women felt excluded and discriminated against (Priest 1997c, WP:
A.01; Sheridan 2003, WP: A.01). Others highlighted how "female" characteristics
made women unable to adapt:

> "I'm sick of hearing about cars and how you're going to soup up your car and
> what you're going to do with your truck," she said, mocking her male
> counterparts. "I don't know what's come over me. I just want to read a good
> home decorating magazine or go shopping."
>
> (Macur 2005, NYT)

Military service masculinizes women

Similar to the last category were statements that dealt with the (necessary)
defeminization of military women (Egan 1996, NYT: A14; Sheridan 2003, WP:
A.01; Britt 2004, WP: B.01). As they were adapting to military life, women
automatically lost their femininity to some extent:

> [She] wears a deep purple suit, gray pearl earrings and a small American flag
> pin in her lapel. She looks normal enough, neither like a rebel nor like some
> military robot type. She is small, with freckles dusting her nose and bangs
> brushing her brows. Her shoulder-length brown hair is pulled back into a
> ponytail. When she walks in her heels, she clomps a little, her shoulders
> leading her feet, maybe from all those hours hunched over the cockpit
> controls.
>
> (Gerhart 2002, WP: C.01)

Military women are cruel

Women's exceptional cruelty was mainly discussed in connection with the Abu
Ghraib torture scandal in 2004. Conservatives constructed the abuse of Iraqi
prisoners by male and female soldiers as "the dark side of integration" and the
involvement of women as evidence for women's general inability to fulfill military
tasks:

> Not every woman is doing a great job, Schlafly said. She said the photograph
> of England holding a leash attached to the neck of an Iraqi prisoner appalled
> her. "This later picture is a feminist fantasy," she said. "That's how feminists
> think about men."
>
> (Phyllis Schlafly, Eagle Forum, in: Fears 2004, WP: A.01)

Women who acted "unwomanly," e.g. by joining the military, had the potential for outrageous, "unnatural" behavior, which had to be prevented by confining women to more suitable environments. Misogynistic thinking was projected onto the enemy and women were held responsible for enraging the Arab world, which was allegedly unable to accept the reversal of gender roles, unlike the US.

Negative statements on military gender integration

Integration hinders military effectiveness

Negative evaluations of integration most often referred to military effectiveness, which played an even larger role here than in positive statements. From the perspective of military efficiency, women were accused of variously impeding military tasks: They reduced readiness due to pregnancies, their responsibility for child-care, and other "biological disabilities" (Nordheimer 1991, NYT: 11; Gellman 1992, WP: a.03), which made military conduct more expensive and complicated (Gutman 1997, NYT: A31). They deteriorated performance standards, were favored (Rohter 1993, NYT: A1), and thus weakened troop cohesion and morale (Schmitt 1991c, NYT: A1). Their presence led to "natural" male behavior involving sexual aggression and competition, which, again, destroyed cohesion among the troops (Schmitt 1991b, NYT: A16; Moore 1991, WP: a.01; Schmitt 1992, NYT: 43; Kreahling 1997, NYT: 13LI8). Despite technological innovations, warfare still required male characteristics, which could not be cultivated when women were present (Editorial 1993, WP: a.20). Integration would thus endanger national security.

> Effectiveness in combat depends on how well soldiers work together. Integrating women in front-line units would irreparably damage that effectiveness. [O]ne of the most important aspects of national security [is] combat effectiveness and [the reason] why women should not be assigned combat duty [is] unit cohesion.
>
> (Editorial 1992, WP: a.21)

In these depictions, supporters of integration were pursuing ideological agendas, while opponents worried about the common good (Lancaster 1992, WP: a.03). Exclusion was argued as pragmatic and rational by constructing a contradiction between military needs and equality (Rayner 1997, NYT: 6/25; Brooke 1997, NYT: A10):

> And what else was to be expected? The military is not a Boy Scout Camporee. It is teaching young people to kill other young people, a work that does not prosper when men are expected to behave like gentlemen and women like ladies.
>
> (Baker 1997, NYT: 119)

Integration is against US values

Another line of argumentation did not doubt women's performance, but claimed that cultural norms would prevent their integration nevertheless (Editorial 1992b, NYT: 118):

> I watched firsthand as American servicewomen performed splendidly there … . But as an experienced combat soldier, I have to say that in direct combat there's something more important than gratitude, more important even than equality and opportunity. It's life and death.
>
> (Hackworth 1991, WP. a.25)

> I believe the combat exclusion law is discrimination against women. And second, that it works to their disadvantage in a career context. I still think it is not a good idea for me to have to order women into combat. Combat is about killing people. I'm afraid that even though logic tells us that women can do that as well as men, I have a very traditional attitude about wives and mothers and daughters being ordered to kill people.
>
> (General McPeak, Airforce Chief of Staff, in: Gordon 1992, NYT: A10)

Others widened this argumentation by insisting on the dangerous consequences that integration would have for general society. The "social experiment" of integration would serve the feminists' goal of achieving a gender-neutral society (Vobejda/Health 1993, WP: A.06). Because of their moral superiority, women should be protected from combat and should not strive for the right to participate in it (Baker 1997, NYT: 119). Sexual abuse, female POWs, shared accommodation for men and women, and mothers as warriors were all issues that were discussed as "moral" problems for society (Baker 1997, NYT: 119; Editorial 1997, WP: A.22; Marcus 2005, WP: A.17). Exclusion was argued as a Western and/or US-American value (Gutman 1997, NYT: A31) that luckily coincided with natural instincts. Integration would destroy the "sexual order of things," which was to be protected from the government's reach (Rayner 1997, NYT: 6/25). The rationality of such argumentation was evaluated differently. While some depicted military efficiency and anti-feminist ideology as inherently intertwined (Gutman 1997, NYT: A31), others spoke of an "uncontrollable protective instinct," which dominated over logic and knowledge of women's abilities. Sexist behavior was thus naturalized. These depictions often mourned for nostalgic masculinist ideals of the past and feared that women's presence would trivialize, demasculinize, and civilize the military, making service just an "ordinary job" (Gutman 1997, NYT: A31).

Integration is a concession to "political correctness"

These statements tried to delegitimize integration by presenting it as a concession to "politically correct" supporters of equality and civil rights and alluding to conspiracy theories. They claimed that military leaders were against integration due to pragmatic reasons, but were suppressed by the civilian leadership (Nordheimer 1991, NYT: 11; Schmitt 1991c, NYT: A1; Lancaster 1992, WP: a.03):

> But conservative Commissioner Ronald D. Ray—like Draude, a Marine Vietnam veteran who was decorated heavily for valor—accused supporters of women's combat roles of being controlled by "politically correct" officials at the Pentagon.
>
> (Gellman 1992, WP: a.03)

"The feminists," who demasculinized the military and wanted to destroy the overall gender order, were a common enemy in these depictions (Mann 1991, WP: d.03). They were pursuing a secret agenda against military men, were unjust, irrational, and powerful (Brooke 1997, NYT: A10). Because of their lobbying, the military had to integrate women against their best knowledge (Priest 1997b, WP: A.13).

The public is against integration

In this category, it was argued that women's abilities and qualifications were less relevant for decisions on further integration than the public's attitudes:

> Pentagon officials said that, setting aside questions about women's strength or suitability for such jobs, they do not believe the American public is ready to send women into ground combat.
>
> (Lancaster 1993, WP: A.01)

"Ordinary soldiers" and "passers-by" were cited who expressed negative attitudes towards women's participation (Ricks 2000, WP: A.03; Wilgoren 2003, NYT: B1), and the Pentagon depicted the current legal situation as a compromise with the public's concerns (Scott Tyson 2005d, WP: A.04). The civilian population was shown as distressed by women's deployment in a war and unable to handle women casualties (Wilgoren 2003, NYT: B1; Cave 2005, NYT: A1). In this view, public opinion had to decide what military roles were acceptable for women.

Women need to be protected

The protection of women, particularly from becoming POW, was one of the most important arguments against integration. Being raped by the enemy was argued as the greatest danger that women faced, greater than torture or death (Sciolino 1990, NYT: A1; Schmitt 1991b, NYT: A16; Sciolino 1992, NYT: A1; Wilgoren 2003, NYT: B1). Though men could be raped, too, women suffered more from it (Vobejda and Health 1993, WP: A.06). Despite their abilities, women had to be excluded from warfare due to these gender-specific dangers. This protective behavior was also argued as a part of the US value system:

> "I love my wife and my daughter," Gillespie told them, adding that having women in combat aviation was "difficult to see … because I've always had this feeling that in this country, the philosophy was that we wouldn't put our women in harm's way."
>
> (Priest 1997a, WP: a.02)

Military service contradicts feminist values

Some statements hinted at the contradiction between women's military participation and feminist-pacifist ideals:

> What kind of society are we when similar opportunity in killing is the standard for equality? Is it an advancement in human development to say that militarists are wrong, that it shouldn't be only males set to slaughtering males—but get females onto the killing fields too?
>
> (McCarthy 1990, WP: f.02)

These statements extended the "protection argument" by demanding that women should be protected from the military's reach and not be turned into perpetrators of violence. Since they were more often victims of warfare, they had the moral responsibility to resist and criticize it (ibid.). Support for integration was portrayed as "perverted feminism" that had strayed from its originally civilizing and sensible ideals (Baker 1997, NYT: 119).

Integration causes sexual abuse

Sexual abuse was constructed as a reason for excluding women, since their presence would naturally lead to sexual violence. Harassment was not caused by institutional discrimination, but by integration (Lancaster 1992, WP: a.03). The only way to protect women was to exclude them, at least from leadership positions (Egan 1996, NYT: A14; Brooke 1997, NYT: A10; Baker 1997, NYT: 119; Rayner 1997, NYT: 6/25):

> Without women in the combat arms, there will never be a proportionate number of female generals. So, do we want more female generals or less sexual harassment? Just acknowledging this trade-off should help clear the air.
>
> (Moskos 1998, WP: C.01)

From this perspective, sexual violence and aggression were also ascribed military functionality:

Military life may correctly foster the attitudes that tend toward rape, such as aggression and single-minded self-assertion. .... In other words, at one level the military's, any military's, existence is perhaps subconsciously predicated on the kind of aggression associated with rape; remove that, and you don't have an army.

(Rayner 1997, NYT: 6/25)

Gender integration is not comparable to racial integration

Arguments for integration that compared gender and racial integration were countered by claims about the gender-specific nature of "bonding," which would transgress ethnic but not the more fundamental gender borders:

[M]ale bonding, a key aspect of unit cohesion, is gender-specific (as is female bonding). .... Today, our effective fighting forces combine males of all races, and the military and the society they serve are the better for it. But the matter of integrating women into combat formations is different because "race" does not equate to "gender."

(Editorial 1992, WP: a.21)

While men were able to assert themselves through performance, women were dependent on "enlightened males" to support their integration (Egan 1996, NYT: A14). Hence, racial integration was compatible with military requirements, while gender integration was not or even contradicted them (Rayner 1997, NYT: 6/25).

The second step: contextualization

The last chapter elaborated the contents of the media discourse on military women and gender integration in the first step of the CHDA. We know now what has been said about these issues in the analyzed media and we have a general idea of the images and arguments used by opponents and supporters of integration in the examined period. We also have an overview of how women and their integration were portrayed in "neutral" descriptions in features and reports, i.e. those that did not openly pursue a particular agenda in debates. What we still do not know is who these opponents and supporters were and why they used the images and arguments they did. Another unknown is the variation of contents in reporting, the changing frequency of different types of statements, and the transformations of ideological constructions used. Clarifying the relationship between military gender ideologies and structural change requires posing these questions. This involves identifying trends in reporting and contextualizing them within the military, social, and political conditions that influence patterns of gender integration. This contextualization constitutes the second step in the CHDA, which includes identifying relevant groups of actors and their interests in processes of social and military change and relating these interests to their argumentative strategies and promoted gender images.

Media debates represent a meta-discourse in which most statements are made by journalists who do not have any direct stakes in military restructuring processes. Additionally, they exert a double influence on trends in reporting because they select the citation from other groups of actors to appear in articles. Comparing the changing relationship between statements from journalists and from outside sources in quantitative and qualitative terms reveals how mainstream attitudes and hegemonic discourses on a certain issue are incorporated into journalistic writing and are then perpetuated and transformed within and by media reporting. It is informative to determine who gets to say what in the media and how much relevance is ascribed to different contributions to the debate. Differing interests are expressed in differing relations between positive and negative statements for each group and in the proportion of statements that each contributed to a specific category. Comparing the relative frequency of different types of statements across actors sheds light on the differences in reasoning for positive or negative evaluations.

The following chapters examine and compare different phases of the period 1990-2005 and investigate the influence of different contextual factors and conditions on reporting content. For a meaningful comparison, the quantitative distribution of articles across that time frame and the general trends in recruitment conditions suggest a separate consideration of three different phases representing different military, social, and political conditions: the early 1990s (phase 1: 1990-1994), the mid-1990s (phase 2: 1995-1999), and the early twenty-first century (phase 3: 2000-2005). Reporting in each phase is examined for the following aspects:

- Distribution of articles across time: How much media attention was given to military gender integration and how were articles distributed across the years?
- Occasions and topics of reporting: Which events and developments drew media attention and initiated reporting? Which did not?
- Relation between positive and negative statement categories: What was the general trend in contents of reporting on the issue?
- Distribution of statements across categories "military women" and "gender integration": Which category received more, which less weight in positive and in negative evaluations? How did arguments and depictions differ in content?
- Relation between different statement groups within positive and negative categories: What were the most frequent arguments in positive and negative discourses? What was the relationship between normative and pragmatic arguments? Which arguments received more, which less opposition?
- Distribution of statements across different groups of actors: How frequently did military, political, and civil society representatives participate in debates? How did they contribute to different statement categories and trends? What were the relations between different statement categories for each group? How did they differ from general trends and from journalists' statements?

- Distribution of statements across genres and newspapers: Where there any significant differences between genres and the two media outlets?

The results pertaining to these questions are related to the social, military, and political contexts of gender integration in each period. Contextual factors to be considered include gender-specific labor division inside and outside the military, civilian and military labor market developments, recruitment situation, strategic and technological conditions, and changing political relations of power globally and within the US. Besides these structural contexts, media debates on military gender issues are also related to discourses on associated issues, such as current interventions, foreign policy, domestic gender policy, and to discourses in fields other than the media, such as inner-military debates, recruitment campaigns, etc. Thereby functions of military gender ideologies in different fields and under different structural and discursive conditions are highlighted.

Professionalized military women in the "Techno War" (phase 1: 1990–1994)

The early 1990s represent a phase in which traditional gender images were most openly questioned in debates on women's military participation. The image of the professional female soldier became the dominant representation, and integration was frequently depicted as efficient and pragmatic. The goal is to explore the structural contexts of these discursive developments. This requires embedding discourses on gender in the military within military restructuring processes after the end of the Cold War and highlighting the impact that these processes have had on recruitment conditions and subsequently on forms and degrees of integration. The functions of gender ideologies in war reporting and propaganda also need to be considered as important contexts shaping representations of military gender issues.

Recruitment conditions and gender integration after the end of the Cold War

Cross-national comparison (Segal 1995) has shown that recruitment conditions exert great influence on patterns of gender integration. It is consequently assumed that they also influence gender ideologies in regard to war and the military. The recruitment environment largely supported women's integration during the first phase of the investigated period and led to a substantial expansion of their military roles. By the early 1990s, warfare technology had raised qualification requirements for new recruits dramatically, causing a lack of qualified specialists. At the same time, the smaller birth cohorts of the late 1960s and early 1970s reached military age. Youth populations, which had reached their peak levels between 1989 and 1991, began to sink again (Armor and Gilroy 2007: 8). Recruitment problems were, however, not primarily of a quantitative nature. Since the break-up of the Soviet Union, US forces had been reduced considerably. Downsizing mostly affected personnel size, which was cut by 100,000 recruits each year between 1989 and 1994 (Warner and Asch 2001: 184). With the recession of the US economy and rising unemployment rates from 1990 to 1992, especially among young Americans, enough personnel were theoretically available to the military (Asch *et al.* 2001: 1ff.). Nevertheless, enlistment dropped by 27 percent in approximately the same time period (Angrist 1995: 1) due to increased demands on qualification levels of recruits. Despite downsizing, the military was struggling to meet recruitment goals and fill its jobs. With the end of the Cold War, it had not turned into a passive entity, but was preparing for a fast intervention in the Persian Gulf since the revolution in Iran (Niva 1998: 117). Recruitment problems were aggravated when the US economy picked up again after 1993. Instead of lowering standards to enable more men to enlist, the legal preconditions to recruit more women were created and their roles expanded (Segal 1995: 766; Warner/Asch 2001: 184). Equality measures were implemented to motivate women to join and stay in the Armed Forces (Asch *et al.* 2001: 15).

The intervention in the Persian Gulf strengthened these trends because it intensified recruitment problems. It was the first large-scale intervention since the Vietnam War and since the establishment of the AVF. It raised women's representation by deploying reserve units, in which women were more strongly represented than among active duty troops. A total of 41,000 women participated in Operation Desert Storm, representing between 7 percent and 8 percent of the troops (Peach 1996: 156; Gabbert 2007: 90f.).[18] Women made up 5.6 percent of enlisted personnel, 12.2 percent of reservists, 7.3 percent of active officers, and 21.3 percent of reserve officers (Segal 1999: 573). A large majority, around 30,000, served in the Army (Brown 2006: 13), where they accounted for 9.2 percent of personnel (Murnane 2007: 1092). Thirteen women were killed in action, two became POW (WREI n.d.). Not only did more women serve in this war, they were also more visible than before. The intense media broadcasting of the intervention revealed to the general public that women had been integrated into the military throughout the past decades and that they were also serving in positions that could not be considered "out of harm's way." War propaganda was also using these images to mobilize the public. Women were taking part in combat (Murnane 2007: 1092) and exclusionary laws posed problems to military readiness and effectiveness (Peach 1996: 174). As a result, the Kennedy-Roth Amendment to the FY 1992–93 Defense Authorization Act permitted women to serve aboard aircraft engaged in combat missions in 1991. Remaining restrictions were now no longer based on the law, but on internal rules of the different services (Stiehm 1996: 159; Murnane 2007: 1094).

The consecutive lifting of discriminatory regulations and new personnel policies were a result of general recruitment conditions and the war in the Gulf. The series of changes in women's legal status between 1991 and 1994 was an acknowledgement of their performance during the intervention, but also a necessity of personnel policy required by recruitment trends and conditions. In addition to these favorable contexts, changes also depended on political power relations. The Clinton administration's first term was marked by a turn towards domestic policy, social and cultural modernization, and the reduction of the national debt and household deficit which had been inherited from President George Bush Senior. Military budgets were cut and money invested in domestic projects. The administration and Secretary of Defense Les Aspin were determined to restructure the military and modernize military culture, which led to increased tension with military elites. Equality for women and homosexuals in the services was one objective of this project. The commitment of the Clinton administration to gender equality in the military and beyond enabled the translation of pressing personnel issues into equality legislature and comprehensive expansion of women's roles.

In 1993 and 1994, Les Aspin advised the Armed Forces to open combat aviation despite recommendations from the *Presidential Commission on the Assignment of Women in the Armed Forces* to uphold exclusions in this area. Additionally, the Navy was to prepare legal measures for lifting the ban on women's assignment to combat vessels. Army and Marines were to investigate further possibilities for opening previously closed positions (WREI n.d.), and the closing of positions in the future was made impossible under the new regulation (Harrell/Miller 1997: 14). Following these directives, the Armed Forces declared that 260,000 new positions were going to be opened to women, most of them on surface combat ships of the Navy and the Marines (Armor 1996: 15). Intelligence, communication, and military police were also opening many positions under the new rules.

The next big step was made in 1994, when the so-called "risk rule" was lifted, which had closed many units in ground combat support to women (Titunik 2008: 6). The newly established "ground combat rule" banned them only from direct involvement in ground combat and thus opened 32,000 new assignments. Since then, 90 percent of assignments in all services have been open to women (Gabbert 2007: 81). In the same year, Congress finally lifted the ban on combat vessels on the surface (Iskra 2007: 204), and Secretary of Defense Aspin ordered integration into combat units on these ships (Gabbert 2007: 81). Following changes in legal conditions, 250,000 combat related jobs, including reserve and National Guard, were opened in 1993/94 (ibid.: 11). Overall, legal reforms had two main consequences for women's participation: first, new positions and assignments were opened, second, eligibility to join units that had been closed by the "risk rule" was established (Harrell and Miller 1997: 4).

Gender ideologies in integration debates

Due to the media spectacle of the Persian Gulf War and the associated lifting of bans on women's participation, the media's interest in military women was high in this phase and peaked in 1991. Almost half of all analyzed articles appeared in the early 1990s (Table 4.2). The lifting of discriminations was the topic on which most articles appeared. But the issue of women at war provided the basis for making these legal changes a media event. Before the Gulf War, in 1990, the intervention in Panama and stationing of female soldiers in the Gulf area already initiated increased media coverage. In 1991, half of all articles dealt with women's

Table 4.2 Distribution of articles across newspapers, genres, and time (phase 1)

	The New York Times				The Washington Post				Total
	Reports	Features	Editorials	Total	Reports	Features	Editorials	Total	
1990	2	0	0	2	1	1	3	5	7
1991	4	4	2	10	3	0	4	7	17
1992	3	0	3	6	2	3	1	6	12
1993	3	1	2	6	2	0	2	4	10
1994	2	0	0	2	1	0	0	1	3
Total	14	5	7	26	9	4	10	23	49

deployment to Operation Desert Storm. Mothers in a war and women casualties were the dominant issues. The other half focused on discriminations and limitations in the services. After the fighting had ceased, reporting on military gender issues declined. The drastic changes implemented in 1994 received scant news coverage. It is highly revealing to investigate not only when the media reported on military women, but also when it did not. Foreign policy events provided the frame and motivation for reporting on gender issues. To a lesser extent, scandals within the military, such as the sexual abuse of Navy women at the Tailhook convention in 1992, inspired media interest. Legal changes alone attracted far less media attention. Reporting ignored military women when covering debates on the ban on homosexuals in the military, though military women in general and homosexual military women in particular are specifically affected by these regulations (Gabbert 2007: 149).

Increased visibility of women's participation and the necessary legal expansion of their military roles are the main contexts for the predominantly positive reporting trend in the analyzed media (Table 4.3). The proportion of positive statements on these issues reached 71 percent and thus peaked during the early 1990s. Military women were portrayed particularly favorably. Positive statements on them accounted for 40 percent of all statements; 31 percent evaluated integration positively, while only 15 percent expressed negative attitudes towards military women and 14 percent towards integration. These general trends were observable in both newspapers: in both, the ratio of positive to negative statements approximated the general relationship. The distribution of positive and negative statements across genres also did not deviate greatly from overall trends. In reports and editorials, positive statements were slightly underrepresented, while they were overrepresented in features. The latter genre worked particularly hard

Table 4.3 Distribution of positive and negative statements (phase 1)

	Positive statements	Negative statements	Total
Military women	40%	15%	55%
Integration	31%	14%	45%
Total	71%	29%	100%

to support the war effort and therefore prominently featured coverage on dutiful service members, including professional and courageous military women.

Uncovering the functionality of gender ideologies in integration debates requires investigating which constructions and arguments were used how often within positive and negative evaluations. For this purpose, the proportion of statement groups within positive and negative categories was compared. The results enable conclusions to be drawn on the capacities in which women were accepted and on the rationales deemed valid for or against integration. Increased acceptance of women in non-combat positions was expressed in an accentuation of their professionalism and the efficiency of their integration. Professionalism was the most frequently featured characterization; it appeared in 19 percent of positive statements on military women. Depictions of female soldiers as courageous (15 percent), emancipated (12 percent), combat-ready (12 percent), and patriotic (11 percent) also occurred comparably frequently. Eight percent claimed that women were already serving in combat and deserved recognition for it. The early 1990s were the only phase in which military service and family were argued as being compatible, in which the right to professional fulfillment was expressed, and in which traditional conceptions of motherliness were contradicted. These claims featured in 8 percent of positive statements on military women.

Among positive statements on integration, military effectiveness was the most prominent (21 percent), but values such as equality, progress, and democracy were also named as arguments and played a larger role within positive versus negative categories. Seventeen percent depicted integration as a necessary step to overcome anachronistic values, and an equal proportion viewed it as a necessary measure to implement the performance principle. Equality was the decisive point of reference in 14 percent of statements. Ten percent argued that the protection argument was invalid and criticized constructions of women as possessions of men. Nine percent depicted integration as a patriotic measure, 6 percent saw war as neutralizing gender differences, and 3 percent argued that public opinion supported integration. In a small number of sporadic statements, gender integration was contextualized within the civil rights movement and the lifting of racist military personnel policies.

The overall positive trend in reporting reflected two groups: journalists and politicians. Statements from journalists constituted a majority (63 percent) of all statements in this phase. Eighty-one percent of these expressed positive attitudes, 50 percent about military women, 31 percent about integration. Journalists contributed 79 percent to all positive statements on military women and 63 percent to all positive statements on integration. They tended to focus more on military women and less on the abstract process of integration. The content of their contributions conformed to the general pattern: professionalism was mentioned most often (18 percent) and leadership qualities least (3 percent) among positive statements on military women. A notable exception from overall trends was the nature of their favorable arguments regarding integration. Unlike other groups of actors, they did not refer to military effectiveness as a main rationale (14 percent), but to the performance principle (21 percent), equality (17 percent), and overcoming of old-fashioned values (15 percent). This features value-oriented argumentations more often than pragmatic ones. Only 19 percent of journalists' statements can be ascribed to negative categories. Twelve percent depicted military women in a negative light, 7 percent argued against integration. Among the first category, most statements (43 percent) focused on the incompatibility of military service and motherhood. Among the second, half of arguments referred to effectiveness, one quarter to protection of women, and the remainder to "political correctness" and public opinion. Journalists still represented the largest group among negative statements on military women (49 percent) and on integration (31 percent). These proportions, however, were relatively low compared to positive categories.

The second group that sustained positive trends were politicians. Since they accounted for only 8 percent of statements during the early 1990s, their influence was lowest of all groups. The cited politicians, however, expressed overwhelmingly positive attitudes. Ninety percent of their statements positively characterized military women or argued in favor of integration. Half of these statements came from the Department of Defense, including DACOWITS and civilian officials in military personnel management. Only Democratic and no Republican Congress members appeared in reporting. Among Senators, no meaningful differences could be observed between Democrats and Republicans. Politicians accounted for 10 percent of positive statements on military women and 11 percent on integration. Not a single statement from politicians expressed negative attitudes towards military women, and only 4 percent of negative statements on integration came from them. Those supporting integration successfully took the lead in media debates. Military women were more often portrayed as courageous than as professional by politicians. The main argument for integration conformed to the general trend, i.e. it referred to military effectiveness. Politicians mainly tried to appeal to US political identity as progressive and democratic to win over the electorate. Even the small number of those who opposed integration did not dare to express negative attitudes towards military women and break the taboo of criticizing the troops. The Democratic hegemony in government and Congress and the administration's commitment to gender equality are mirrored in these results, but also the broad pro-integration consensus between both parties due to the war in the Gulf.

Due to the differing interests of political and military elites, integration remained a conflictuous process facing resistance from many angles. During the early 1990s, opponents were voicing their opinions and organizing to resist new legislation. As a concession to the critics in the Senate, the *Presidential Commission on the Assignment of Women in the Armed Forces* was established in 1991. It included only two representatives of the military and many renowned conservative opponents of integration (Murnane 2007: 1094). In an eight to seven vote in 1992, the commission demanded a re-establishment of the ban on aerial combat and the permanent exclusion from ground combat. However, the first recommendation was unheeded. Under the military and political conditions of the era, opponents were unable to fully enforce their interests.

It would nonetheless be an overstatement to assume that opponents had no impact on legislation and associated debates. Partly due to their resistance, integration remained limited. The expansion of women's roles was primarily designed to serve the military's needs and thus adapted to its personnel requirements. Integration into previously closed non-combat positions was enabled, particularly in ground combat support, where demand for qualified personnel was most pressing. The exclusion from direct ground combat was upheld because these units were less affected by the lack of specialist personnel; women remained excluded from "all assignments that involve operating offensive, line-of-sight weapons and from all positions entailing ground fighting," including "armor, infantry, and field artillery" (Peach 1996: 159). These new rules fulfilled the same functions as the "risk rule" had before: Women could be integrated into areas in which they were needed, but excluded from others for which enough men competed.

These exclusions still have discriminatory effects on military women and their careers. While they often face the same dangers as actual combat troops, particularly in combat support, they do not have the same status that goes along with combat positions (Peach 1996: 159). Combat exclusion not only entails disadvantages in terms of pay, but also negates certain training and educational programs as well as insurance and credit benefits. Professional advancement is curtailed because many leadership positions require combat experience. This translates into disadvantages on the civilian labor market compared with male veterans (ibid.: 175). Female officers have a harder time acquiring the leadership qualifications that are useful for military and civilian careers alike (Gabbert 2007: 84). Besides these legal impediments, assignment policies hinder equal integration. Though women were accepted to the newly opened units, they were mostly assigned to jobs in administration, in which they could not acquire necessary qualifications for promotion (Harrell and Miller 1997: 31). Integration was thus also regulated and de facto limited by assignment practices.

Conflicts on integration, and resistance against it, affected media discourses on military gender issues and the ideologies expressed therein. Many statements featured negative stereotypes about military women and rejected integration. Opponents used prejudice against women as mentally unstable and programmed to preserve life. They also argued that their presence impeded or even hindered fulfilling military tasks. Arguments regarding effectiveness were even more dominant within negative than within positive categories: they featured in 37 percent of negative statements on integration. Based on demographic changes in personnel structure[19], the issue of mothers in the military was instrumentalized to delegitimize participation. Depictions of military women as inadequate mothers were the most frequent depictions and featured in 32 percent of negative statements on military women. One discursive context was the ban on the recruitment of married Marines, which was installed by the Marine Corps leadership, but later repealed by the Pentagon.

Depictions of mental unfitness for service were also relatively prevalent (26 percent). In comparison, prejudice about physical inadequacy appeared relatively infrequently, namely in 14 percent of statements. Similar proportions claimed that women did not want to serve in combat, and 12 percent referred to military men's retention against integration as a relevant reason for exclusion. Among negative statements on integration, 16 percent argued for exclusion for women's own protection. Twelve percent constructed exclusion as a (US) value, and an equal proportion devalued integration as a concession to "political correctness". The smallest groups of arguments related to public opinion and sexual abuse as rationales for exclusion (both 6 percent). Ten percent of negative statements on integration also objected out of pacifist/feminist motives. These critiques sometimes included traditional conceptions of women as "beautiful souls." Adapting integration to suit military demands not only determined the share and contents of negative statements, but also the nature of positive ones. Most debates centered on limited integration, rarely on absolute equality. Accordingly, leadership qualities were seldom ascribed to military women and only featured in 2 percent of positive statements on them. They were also portrayed as reliable comrades on the battlefield in only 5 percent of statements. These categories correspond to the positions that remained closed: leadership positions and ground combat troops.

While political representatives supported integration by a large majority, the military often spoke out against overtly ambitious equality measures. Its representatives accounted for 13 percent of all statements. Though this value is modest, the military was given more room in media reporting than political representatives. Fifty-nine percent of the military's statements were negative. Twenty-two percent depicted integration and 38 percent military women negatively. Among negative statements on military women, the military accounted for 20 percent, among negative statements on integration 35 percent. In the latter category, the military was the largest group of proponents. Almost half of negative statements featured effectiveness as the major obstacle to integration. One third of them stem from the Air Force. The rest were equally distributed across Army, Navy, and Marines. Only 10 percent of the military's statements depicted integration and only 20 percent military women positively. These smaller groups of statements referred to professionalism and military effectiveness in most instances. Half of them came from the Marines, followed by the Navy and the Army. Only one came from the Air Force. The military accounted for 13 percent of positive statements on integration and only 3 percent of those on military women. Note the military's statements were mostly negative, even though integration helped solve recruitment problems. Absolute equality, as occasionally demanded from outside, meant complete deregulation and increased competition in all areas, which was not in the interest of military personnel management.

A main context for the military's participation in media debates is provided by the changing power relations between military and civilian leadership during the Clinton era. The relationship between the Armed Forces and the administration was shaped by power struggles, particularly after the presentation of the Pentagon's vision for the military after the Cold War in the summer of 1993. The Armed Forces were to be significantly smaller, restructured and adapted to regional conflicts. With these measures, Clinton planned on saving $88 billion more on the military budget than his predecessor had planned. The long-standing strategic concept which required the military to be able to engage in two wars at the same time was abolished and substituted by a "win-hold-win" doctrine. The administration was of the opinion that military responsibility was to be shared in the post-Cold-War world. But already at the beginning of Clinton's first term, Congress and military leaders opposed this position. Because strategic and budgetary reform produced winners and losers, struggles over power and budget within the military were enhanced as well. Army, Navy, and Air Force were reduced, while the Marines grew in personnel. The Navy particularly suffered from cuts on aerial weaponry which impeded its participation in far away conflicts. As a consequence, the Air Force gained in importance. The Marine Corps which had competed with the Army for the lead role as main Quick Reaction Force prevailed.

Further tension between military and civilian leadership was introduced by gender-related issues. Aside from women's integration, the administration threatened hegemonic military masculinity by promising to remove restrictions on homosexuals in the service. The Federal Appeals Court had declared the exclusion of homosexuals illegal. Introduction of new rules in this regard was met with staunch resistance, particularly from the Joint Chiefs of Staff and Republican representatives. Republican senator Sam Nunn, chairman of the Senate Armed Services Committee, demanded that any new regulations expressed the incomparability of military and civilian life. Arguments were quite similar to those against military women: Homosexual troops were portrayed as an unacceptable risk to morale, cohesion, and discipline. Their integration would impede recruitment, cause religious soldiers to leave the services, promote promiscuity, and increase the risk of HIV infections for heterosexuals. By supporters of the ban, homosexuality was largely constructed as an aberration from military masculinity ideals. A compromise was reached, known as the "don't ask, don't tell" policy. According to it, homosexuals may serve, but must not act out or speak about their sexual orientation. The military is also not allowed to ask recruits about their sexuality. More tension was added to the civilian–military relationship, when the Marines' leadership prohibited the recruitment of married troops, which the administration revised later. The Clinton administration was thus not only responsible for the drastic cuts in military budgets and the controversial strategic reorientation, but also for the modernization of traditional military culture and its masculinist values. Military representatives thus widely perceived the "new world order" under Clinton as a power loss and a demasculinization.

Due to the different effects of military reform on each service, the military is by no means a unified actor in integration debates. Breaking down the statements into the four services, however, yields very small numbers that hamper a meaningful interpretation. Analysis of recruitment campaigns (Brown 2006) has shown that all services make use of gender ideologies. Variations in these ideologies are informative about patterns of inclusion and exclusion in each service because they reflect the different affectedness by technologization and professionalization and the proportion of higher-qualified jobs to be filled with women. During the early 1990s, Army and Navy campaigns focused on more gender-neutral aspects, such as self-fulfillment and training in technical skills that are useful for civilian careers. Services less affected by modernization processes, such as the Marines, still advertised exclusive and elitist masculinity using catchwords such as "pride" and "challenge." The positions on integration, as presented in media debates, cannot be directly deduced from gender ideologies used in campaigns or even from women's representation in the respective service. In the early 1990s, the service with the highest female participation, the Air Force, was the most negative group; the Marines, with the lowest rate, were the most positive. The differing functions of gender ideologies in integration debates are investigated further in the following chapters. These rely on more data on the participation of the military and its forces in media debates and make comparisons across the whole period of investigation. The influential factors on the promoted gender ideologies are not only each service's demand for the female workforce, but also recruits' demand for jobs within the respective service.

An even greater contribution to negative trends was made by representatives of civil society, who accounted for 14 percent of all statements, including those criticizing integration for feminist or pacifist reasons. Their participation was negative by a majority of 62 percent and mostly stemmed from interest groups, which professionally organized against integration. Civil society representatives played a particularly large role in negative depictions of integration; their statements accounted for 29 percent in this category. Among negative statements on military women, theirs made up 7 percent. Their participation in the positive categories was low: 22 percent featured positive portrayals and arguments about integration, and only 15 percent about military women. As such, they accounted for only 5 percent within the first and 10 percent within the latter category. The majority of these positive statements came from authors, scientists, and intellectuals who did not appear as official representatives of organizations. They depicted women's military exclusion as a problem of old-fashioned values and less often referred to effectiveness.

Gender ideologies in war reporting

Fully understanding the nature and transformation of military gender ideologies requires considering their functions on two levels: within debates on integration, and within related discourses, most importantly on current interventions as they were featured in war reporting. War is both a discursive and structural context. It strongly influences recruitment conditions and the gender-specific labor division. As such, it is one cause of enhanced integration and can lead to positive trends in media discourses on military women. In later chapters that compare the Persian Gulf War to the "War on Terror," it is evident that reporting is not only influenced by whether the US forces are involved in a war, but also by how the particular war is discursively processed. This, in turn, depends on political and strategic conditions of warfare, global power relations, and objectives in foreign as well as domestic policy. For the early 1990s, the Persian Gulf War and the UN intervention in Somalia provide important contexts for the instrumentalization of gender ideologies. Representations of both events utilized modern as well as traditional gender images; even though borders between masculinity and femininity ideals were shifting, the frameworks for interpreting war remained heavily gendered.

Developments on the news media market also need to be considered in the analysis of war reporting in the early 1990s. The economic decline and subsequent privatization of many media companies, increased competition on the media market, and technological innovations in communication and warfare deepened the reciprocal relationship of dependency between the media and the military, fostering uncritical reporting and propagandistic images of war (Jeffords/ Rabinovitz 1994: 2ff.). The Persian Gulf War was the first to be broadcasted live on TV. However, journalists' access to the theater of war was strictly controlled. Reports had to be presented to military representatives before they could be published (ibid.: 11). The pool system, which became the norm of reporting, led to a high degree of dependency of journalists on the military and excluded smaller media outlets:

> The combination of security review and the use of the pool system as a form of censorship made the Gulf War the most uncovered major conflict in modern American history … . Our sense is that virtually all major news organizations agree that the flow of information to the public was blocked, impeded or diminished by the policies and practices of the Department of Defense.
>
> (Dunsmore 1996: 5f.)

During Operation Desert Storm, the image of the Armed Forces as portrayed by the mainstream media was that of a high-tech military fighting with a new professional ethos and led by modern managers (Mariscal 1991: 106). The intervention itself was constructed as a clean, modern "Techno War" of "surgical" attacks commanded by a corporate military. War reporting concentrated on technological superiority of the US forces. Aerial warfare played a major role, and propaganda and media hype additionally sharpened the focus on technological aspects, diverting attention from infantry soldiers (and civilian victims) to battle tank commanders and high-tech pilots. These strategic and discursive contexts led to a shift in gender ideologies, establishing a "new world order masculinity" (Niva 1998). Traditional images of the male combatant were replaced by images of the qualified specialist. "[T]hose appropriately equipped and educated for new world order warfare" (ibid.: 120) served as a new model of identification for middle- and upper-class men.

Military and civilian masculinity stereotypes were also supplemented by "female" qualities, and war reporting showed military representatives and civilian leaders as hyper-efficient, but also as sensitive and compassionate (ibid.: 130f.).

These shifts were a reaction to changing gender relations in the US, but also to the new role of the USA in an increasingly unipolar world, in which it presented itself as a role model for emancipation and equality. In this scenario, the enemy was portrayed as an uncivilized hyper-macho, while Western masculinity was idealized as "tough and tender" (ibid.: 119). The media presence of military women and depictions of their participation supported images of cooperative, open-minded US masculinity and generated support for the intervention. In this context, emancipated female soldiers were often featured in the examined media, and integration was argued as a logical consequence of US progressivism and moral superiority.

Images of aggressive, individualistic, competitive, and adventurous women matched conceptions of modern technological and professionalized warfare (Gabbert 2007: 103f.). New technologies were supposed to make war a gender-neutral phenomenon and produce a unisex warrior ethos. Individual qualities were revalued in relation to group characteristics. These neo-liberal ideas were also expressed within the analyzed material: Collective affiliations such as gender and liberal values such as equality took only second place to arguments referring to performance. Individual achievement became a key concept, analogous to the civilian labor market, to which the military was supposed to conform. Consequently, professionalism, efficiency, qualification, expertise, and discipline were most often highlighted as positive characteristics of military women. This does not mean, however, that traditional gender ideologies completely lost their functionality in war reporting and propaganda. Stereotypically female characteristics were used in depictions of the home front, on which the national community was awaiting the homecoming of the war heroes (Mariscal 1991: 103f.). The war in the Persian Gulf was also often associated with the overcoming of the "Vietnam syndrome" and the reattainment of heroic masculinity, which was believed to having been lost in this war.

Similar remasculinizing tendencies were observable in media representations of the US-led UN mission in Somalia. Military women were much less of an issue here, but coverage made use of gender ideologies in other ways. A case study of NYT reporting on the events in Mogadishu on 3 October 1993 shows that coverage was deeply gendered, though none of the search keys used for the general study applied to articles on these events. When the Bush Senior administration offered to send troops to Somalia in a multinational intervention to stop a massive famine, it had aimed at a televised military success comparable to the Gulf War. As the troops arrived on the Somali coast in December 1992, they were greeted by cameras and reporters and their landing was presented as a great TV spectacle, symbolizing the advent of the "new world order." Though the intervention had been justified as a "humanitarian" action to relieve the famine, Somalia soon proved to be a highly complex military and political challenge. There was little consensus on how to take it on under the conditions of increasing tensions between military leadership and the new Clinton administration. In accordance with the new multilateral military doctrine, Clinton handed the command of the operation over to the UN in May 1993, which was unprecedented in US military history and increased domestic criticism of the mission. On October 3, Special Forces were sent on a secret mission to arrest local warlord General Aidid. The mission failed and the troops were involved in 15-hour combat operations with Somali militia. Two helicopters were shot down, 18 soldiers killed, and over 70 wounded. In the aftermath of the fighting, Somali forces dragged the bodies of killed US soldiers through the streets of Mogadishu. The images of this incident were broadcasted all around the world. As a reaction to the public outcry, Clinton sped up the withdrawal of troops until March 1994, when all US troops left Somalia.

Gender ideologies played a central role in evaluations of the mission and were employed to support the preferred version of the war narrative. Before October 3, media representations instrumentalized traditional stereotypes to generate support for the war and focused on men and women who conformed to them. This affected portrayals of men and women, both Somali and American. Though about 1,000 US military women took part in this mission, US women appeared only as self-sacrificing military wives, grieving widows, and mothers and sisters of war heroes. Female soldiers received little to no media attention, because they were not serving in ground combat, which was of central strategic importance, and outside of the spectacular Special Forces units, which played the lead role in the drama of the rescue of US pilot Michael Durant. Media coverage highlighted "exceptional heroism" (Associated Press 1993, NYT: 1/29) and "camaraderie on the battlefield" (Gordon 1993, NYT: C1), when describing these male heroes. Somali women were also portrayed in traditional ways and were used to proof the enemy's cruelty. Though many participated actively in the fighting, media representations featured them in stereotypical roles: victims of violence, peaceful wives of warriors, and heroic nurses. While Somali men mainly appeared as anonymous, irrational masses, stories on the suffering of individual Somali women were used to justify the "humanitarian intervention." The US was supposed to save these women and help them achieve equality. Consequently, the relationship between the US and Somalia was also described in gendered codes. The US was constructed as the noble savior, Somalia as the obstreperous, but helpless "damsel in distress." The intervention was frequently legitimized by reference to a male codex of honor:

> The Somalis were courted, but instead of roses, the beloved was given heavy armaments . . . . The risk to President Clinton is great. But there is something noble about a large and powerful country saving a million lives in a small and troubled one.
>
> (Herbert 1993, NYT: 4/15)

After the events of October 3, the media switched to evaluations of the mission as "failed" and demanded the withdrawal of troops from Somalia. Hallin (1984) showed that the media generally supports decisions and courses of political elites, as long as there is a significant level of unity among hegemonic social groups. During the Persian Gulf War, the military and the government jointly controlled the circulation of information, and the mass media generated support for the war effort. This successful staging of the "Techno War" could not be repeated for the Somalia intervention because conflicts of interest between military and civilian leadership arose on the course of foreign policy and the role of the Armed Forces after the Cold War. The symbiosis between media, government, and military elites could not be upheld. Differences in media representations were also caused by strategic conditions. Aerial warfare was central to the Persian Gulf War. This had allowed for extended control over media reporting, because independent research and verification of information was almost impossible. The sterile image of the heroic "Techno War" could not be sustained for the Somalia intervention. Instead of precise air strikes on radars, the public was confronted with the images of dead US soldiers, dragged through the streets by triumphant Somali forces.

After the fighting on October 3, perspectives of military leaders and Republican representatives dominated media reporting. Republican opposition used the incidents to proof the government's lack of military and foreign policy leadership and enforce their vision for the military's future: no multilateral interventions, no sharing of military control with the UN. The handing over of command to the UN was held responsible for the defeat, despite the fact that the central units of the Quick Reaction Force and the Army Rangers had constantly been under US command. Only support troops were led by UN commanders. Struggles over the military doctrine after the Cold War were won by those who supported a more isolationist course. Gender ideologies attained new functions in this phase of the mission and were particularly used to delegitimize the Clinton administration's policies on Somalia and its military policy in general, including the introduction of multilateralism, budget cuts, and gender integration. Conflicts of interest between military and civilian leadership were coded in gendered terms: An active, determined, and aggressive military was juxtaposed to a passive, weak political apparatus. The media began to compare the intervention to the Vietnam War, claiming that US military power was again endangered by a feminized civilian leadership. The government had again robbed the individual male soldiers of their deserved status as war heroes. The defeat at Mogadishu was interpreted as a deheroizing of war and demasculinization of the US military. In this context, lost masculinity was related to military modernization and women's integration:

> For generations of American warriors, there has never been much of a question: the essence of soldiering is fighting and winning. ... The warriors of the future will also include computer nerds and intelligence geeks. ... Suddenly buying blankets and combat boots is a lot sexier. ... In today's grudgingly politically correct military, an officer's record on opening opportunities for women also counts towards promotion. The new emphasis has opened new doors for women themselves—ushering in female fighter pilots and warship officers.
>
> (Schmitt 1993, NYT: 4/5)

Gender ideologies were also utilized in describing the relationship between the US and the UN. "Female" duties and abilities were often ascribed to the UN, which was portrayed as unwilling to take responsibility, passive, and weak, while the US was associated with "masculine" traits such as courage, daringness, and toughness. It was frequently argued that the UN should concentrate on diplomatic and peace-keeping operations and leave military decisions to the US. The manifold problems and conflicts of competence during the Somalia mission were coded in terms and images associated with a battle of the sexes, in which the female part tries to take over male tasks and thus needs to be put back in place:

> [T]he military has never been comfortable in the comfort business. It is in the business of getting the job done. ... There are organizations that feed people, and organizations that do battle with them. Together they make an uneasy, perhaps impossible marriage.
>
> (Quindlen 1993, NYT: A29)

An "unmanly" military was claimed to be unable to succeed against the archaic masculinity of the villain, Somali leader Mohammed Farah Aidid. Between the extremes of bureaucratic, feminized UN masculinity, and brutal, uncivilized Somali masculinity, the US was positioned as the masculine ideal of rationality and assertiveness.

After the "surgical interventions" of the high-tech war in the Gulf, the Somalia mission destroyed the belief in the possibility of war without (US) casualties. The dissolution of the bipolar world order, combined with military defeat, supported conclusions that US military power must not be shared and that the Armed Forces should not be utilized in "humanitarian" interventions. Loss of power to the civilian leadership and the altered military role as a UN peacekeeper provided the main frames for interpreting the intervention. These conditions led to idealization of a heroic, masculine war of the past, despite the generally positive attitudes towards military women that were expressed in the media during the same time period. While the glorious victory in the Gulf had been accompanied by overwhelmingly positive depictions of women in service, defeat, loss of the military's power, competition within the military as well as between military and civilian leadership, and an intervention that was based on ground combat troops and Special Forces led to the dissemination of more traditional gender ideologies just a few years later. Including this case study shows that the general selection criteria for the study tend to exclude gendering of reporting that does not explicitly focus on military women. The results on integration debates thus need to be complemented by these findings on gender ideologies in other discursive contexts, such as war reporting.

Sexualized intruders into the male bond (phase 2: 1995–1999)

By the late 1990s, reporting on military gender issues had changed considerably, both quantitatively and qualitatively, compared to the earlier years of the decade. Depictions of military women turned from being mostly positive to mostly negative. These transformations were caused by downsizing, competition for remaining jobs, absence of major interventions, and altered power relations after the "Republican Revolution" in Congress. The implementation of equality measures, which had been introduced during the early 1990s, had raised rates of female participation at a time when many (male) jobs were lost. Under these conditions, military women and their integration were portrayed overwhelmingly negatively in media discourses. Reporting on integration generally declined and was substituted by intense media coverage of "sex scandals" within the military.

Gender integration on competitive military job markets

During the mid-1990s, downsizing was continued. Fewer new personnel were admitted than would have been necessary in order to maintain the numbers already in service (Asch *et al.* 2001: 1). By the late 1990s, the military stood at two thirds of its pre-1990 size. Active troops were affected by downsizing more than the reserves. Reserve units attained a more important role in the overall strategic concept, explaining why their size (about 877,000 troops) approximated the numbers before 1973 (Warner and Asch 2001: 177). Since women are over-represented among reservists, downsizing generally affected those parts of the military with lower female participation rates more.

The legal status of women in the military did not change significantly during this period, but their proportion grew due to implementation of integration measures in the early 1990s (Table 3.1). Unlike in earlier decades, downsizing did not lower women's participation (Gabbert 2007: 280). The Navy saw an increase from 14 percent to 20 percent female enlisted between 1992/93 and 1994/95, the Army from 16 percent to 19 percent, and the Air Force from 22 percent to 24 percent (Armor 1996: 14f.). Among officer ranks, 14 percent were women, among new officers 19 percent (Warner and Asch 2001: 186). During Operation Desert Fox in 1998, the Air Force assigned female pilots to combat positions for the first time to secure the no-fly zone over Iraq (Brown 2006: 30). Between 1996 and 2001, 15,000 military women served in Bosnia; between 1999 and 2001, 8,000 served in Kosovo (WREI n.d.). Due to relaxed combat exclusion rules, around 90 percent of occupations were technically open to women. The proportion of actually available jobs was, however, significantly lower in some services due to ground combat exclusions: Only 62 percent of jobs were open within the Marine Corps and 70 percent within the Army (Segal *et al.* 1998: 66). Women were still overrepresented in traditionally "female" occupations: 33 percent of enlisted women and 14.9 percent of female officers served in administration, and 15.6 percent of enlisted women and 46.5 percent of female officers served in health care (Segal 1999: 571).

Strong representation at a time of severe job cutbacks nurtured new anti-integration sentiments. On the structural level, formal and informal measures leveled off the steep increase in women's participation, which evened out at 14 percent of active troops by 1998 (Segal *et al.* 1998: 66) and ranged from 18 percent in the Air Force and 5.4 percent in the Marine Corps (Warner and Asch

2001: 186). This reduction was further promoted by new limitations introduced in 1999 and 2000. Per Department of Defense regulation, costs associated with integration could be used to deny women's entry into Navy ships. The 2001 Defense Authorization Bill even prohibited the Navy from spending money to reconfigure or design submarines to accommodate women and from assigning them to submarines without Congressional approval (Iskra 2007: 212f.). Assignment practices also kept newly opened positions closed and impeded promotion to higher ranks (Harrell and Miller 1997: 31).

Increased sexual violence against military women perpetrated by their male colleagues was one reaction to increased female participation. Sexual harassment and abuse increase when female representation rises and when opportunities are enhanced for women within an institution, but equal status is not awarded completely (Segal 1999: 575). Sexual violence is more frequent in those work fields in which men's overall proportion is high and/or in which leadership is dominated by men. Moreover, tolerance for sexual abuse is more widespread there (Vogt *et al.* 2007: 879). These conditions were present in the military during the 1990s and led to a number of public scandals. In 1996, sexual abuse of female recruits by a male Army Drill Sergeant at the Aberdeen Proving Ground became public, and the Navy was also struggling with cases of "inappropriate" sexual relationships between service members. "Sexual misconduct" became a central issue of media reporting, but also provided the basis for governmental action in regard to military gender issues. Following the Aberdeen scandal, Secretary of Defense William Cohen introduced a panel on gender-integrated training. It produced the *Report of the Federal Advisory Committee on Gender-Integrated Training and Related Issues to the Secretary of Defense*. Though it generally evaluated integration positively, it recommended separate basic training (Titunik 2000: 231). The anti-integration lobby supported this recommendation and portrayed the Marines as a role model in this regard. Their low women's proportion and gender-separated training were associated with their success in attracting sufficient recruits (Brown 2006: 32). However, recommendations to separate male and female recruits in the early stages of training were not realized for the other services.

The 1994 Republican victory in Congressional elections marked a major change in political conditions of integration. The Republican majority during a time without major military interventions meant power gains for political and military opponents of the Clinton administration's modernization of military gender policies. Though legal conditions were not significantly altered, the political atmosphere had changed; this supported anti-integration sentiments and negative attitudes towards military women. This was reflected in negative reporting campaigns. The relative success of supporters and opponents of integration is, however, difficult to measure in terms of policy outcomes. Both groups attained minor victories, but none of them seriously affected the legal status quo. A 1997 Pentagon report to Congress (Harrell and Miller 1997) generally evaluated integration into newly opened positions favorably; no recommendations for changes in the legal status of military women were included.

Opponents were unable to re-establish bans on participation, but political interventions to improve the situation of women were also unsuccessful, because they were not supported by recruitment demands or the political majority within the legislative. Debates on the deployment to Navy submarines serve as an example. Debates were initiated by DACOWITS. The Navy was not keen on this integration due to submarine renovation costs and to the decreased demand for female workforce. As a consequence, it did not fight legislature that limited its flexibility in this regard (Iskra 2007: 212f.). DACOWITS was unable to enforce its demand for revaluation of exclusions and to initiate public debate. The related policy changes hardly made it into the news.

In the later 1990s, new recruitment shortages arose, which were aggravated by declining youth populations, which reached a low in 1996 (Armor/Gilroy 2007: 8), and by the increasing strength of the US economy. Civilian unemployment was comparably low (Warner and Asch 2001: 170) and declined 29 percent between 1993 and 1996 (Asch *et al.* 2001: 11). Real wages of 18- to 24-year-old high school graduates were rising, causing military wages to sink 10 percent in comparison (Warner and Asch 2001: 185). With the impeded recruitment situation starting in 1997/98, anti-integration sentiments were mitigated in media report-ing. Beginning in 2000, integration was again advertised as a solution to recruitment problems (Asch *et al.* 2001: 11).

Gender ideologies in integration debates

Under the recruitment conditions and political power relations in the second half of the 1990s, media attention for military gender issues declined sharply, as clearly evident in Table 4.4. Only 18 percent of analyzed articles were published in this phase. A large majority of these appeared in 1997. For the remaining years, a maximum of only one or two articles per year met the selection criteria. Since recruitment problems do not suffice to inspire the media's interest in integration, reporting was also low during the shortages of the late 1990s. The next peak in reporting first came with the "War on Terror." But not only the quantity of articles had changed, their topics had as well. In the context of increasing cases of sexual harassment, the media became preoccupied with incidents of sexual violence and relationships between service members. In reporting on these issues, they

Table 4.4 Distribution of articles across newspapers, genres, and time (phase 2)

	The New York Times				The Washington Post				Total
	Reports	Features	Editorials	Total	Reports	Features	Editorials	Total	
1995	0	0	0	0	0	0	0	0	0
1996	1	1	0	2	0	0	0	0	2
1997	4	2	2	8	4	0	1	5	13
1998	0	0	0	0	0	0	1	1	1
1999	1	0	0	1	0	0	0	0	1
Total	6	3	2	11	4	0	2	6	17

primarily featured women in the role of victims. Though many media outlets took sides with the abused women and demanded the persecution of the perpetrators, they often constructed female service members as helpless and in need of media support (Hanson 2002). Reporting on various "sex scandals" was intense, but did not often relate these to integration processes, explaining why many such articles were excluded from the sample. Reporting on "sex scandals" did, however, provide an important discursive context for integration debates and hence also influenced the images of military women within these.

These shifts in the quantity and topics of reporting were accompanied by changes in the contents of discourses. This time, the media featured overwhelmingly negative representations. The relationship between positive and negative statement categories nearly reversed, with 60 percent negative statements (Table 4.5). The formerly smallest category (negative statements on military women) had become the largest (42 percent). Eighteen percent expressed negative attitudes towards integration. Seventeen percent referred positively to military women. This latter group, which had previously been the largest, now represented the smallest category. Positive statements on integration still constituted the second largest group at 23 percent. Debates increasingly focused on the process of integration, and the widespread consensus was that it was harmful to the military and to society. Female service members were pushed to the background of media discourses and only few statements had anything good— or even bad—to say about them. Nonetheless, this negative media campaign began to wear off after 1997, when new recruitment shortages arose. The end of the millennium already marks the transition to the next "positive" phase. Note that the negative trend in reporting was caused by a decline in positive statements rather than by an increase in negative ones, which seem to represent the greater constant.

During the mid-1990s, significant differences existed between both newspapers in quantitative and qualitative terms (Table 4.5). The NYT published almost twice as many articles as the WP; 69 percent of statements appeared in the NYT. More importantly, the relationship between negative and positive statements differed substantially. While statements were almost equally distributed across negative and positive categories in the WP (51 percent positive), 69 percent of the NYT's statements were negative. Since the latter published a larger proportion of articles in this period, the negative trend was enhanced for all reporting. The decrease in positive statements was also an effect of the distribution of articles across genres and reflected the absence of a major military intervention. Military activity had previously inspired many features on life on military bases and on the home front,

Table 4.5 Distribution of positive and negative statements (phase 2)

	Positive statements	*Negative statements*	*Total*
Military Women	17%	42%	59%
Integration	23%	18%	41%
Total	40%	60%	100%

which had tended to portray military women more positively. Even during the later 1990s, the features were reporting positively on gender issues by majority (55 percent). However, this genre became less frequent; not a single feature on military gender issues appeared in the WP. In reports and editorials, which were now the dominant genres, negative statements had been more strongly represented in earlier periods as well. This was even more the case now. Within reports, which were the most frequent genre in both newspapers, negative descriptions featured in 65 percent of statements. An even stronger overrepresentation of negative evaluations occurred in editorials (79 percent). Within this more opinionated genre a very strong negative consensus existed.

The general relationship between positive and negative representations had shifted, but also the contents of argumentation strategies within both categories. Value-oriented argumentations were strengthened and normative arguments increased in relation to pragmatic ones. Supporters of integration named gender equality, which featured in 31 percent of positive statements on integration, most frequently as a reason to include women. Military effectiveness only reached second place at 25 percent. Opponents still most often referred to military effectiveness (31 percent), but here, too, arguments depicting exclusion as a cultural value increased from 12 percent in the early 1990s to 20 percent. Seventeen percent saw sexual violence as a valid reason for exclusion and 16 percent portrayed integration as a result of forced "political correctness," as opposed to 6 percent and 12 percent respectively in the early 1990s. The importance of women's protection declined, as did feminist and pacifist conceptions, which were both only mentioned sporadically. Public opinion disappeared as a point of reference from argumentations of both sides. The general public and its attitudes were no longer considered a valid argument. Military effectiveness and cultural norms were to decide upon women's status, and not democratic processes and populist appeals. The few statements which still described military women favorably focused on professionalism and courage. Depictions of professional female soldiers were the most frequent positive statements on military women (31 percent). Nineteen percent portrayed them as courageous. Positive statements on military women were thus the only group to maintain the primacy of pragmatic arguments.

Overall, discourses were highly biologistic: arguments against integration as well as depictions of military women frequently referred to biological and sexual "obstacles" to equality. Many statements claimed that motherhood and military service were incompatible and that women were unwilling to engage in combat. Depictions of service members as "bad" mothers featured in 36 percent of negative statements on military women, those of women refusing to serve in combat in 17 percent. The formerly frequent stereotypes of physical and mental unfitness were only represented marginally. Darlene Iskra (2007) suggests that debates were "sexualized" within the military as well. During the 1970s and early 1990s, pregnancy and sexuality had been mentioned rarely as reasons to exclude women within Navy debates. During the late 1990s, such arguments came to play a major role in debates on integration onto submarines.

Transformations also occurred in regard to the participation of different groups of actors. The negative overall trend was now caused by journalists and politicians, the same groups that had been responsible for the positive trend in the early 1990s, and by civil society representatives. Statements from this latter group became much more influential in this period, reducing journalists' contributions to 55 percent. Compared to earlier years, the relationship between positive and negative categories had also shifted for journalists. Now, a majority of 54 percent of their statements were negative. Most frequently, they spoke negatively about integration (33 percent). One third of these statements referred to efficiency and another third to exclusion as a normatively required measure, making pragmatic and normative arguments equally strong within this group of actors. Twenty-one percent of their statements were negative portrayals of military women, with depictions as deficient mothers being the most frequent content within this category (39 percent). Twenty percent of journalists' statements referred positively to integration. Among these statements, equality was the most often used argument (29 percent). Twenty-four percent referred to effectiveness and an equal proportion to war as gender-neutral. Journalists tended to maintain rather positive attitudes towards military women, as this category remained the second largest among their statements (26 percent). Professionalism and courage were the most frequently featured descriptions, accounting for 23 percent each within this statements category. Journalists contributed 84 percent to positive statements on military women, but only 47 percent to positive statements on integration. Sixty-four percent of negative statements on women and 44 percent of negative ones on integration came from journalists.

The most significant shift from a positive towards a negative majority was observed within the group comprising the political representatives. Their statements made up only 5 percent of the total and had thus further declined. One hundred percent of these statements were negative and all were on integration (none on military women). Political representatives had not expressed any negative attitudes towards female service members in the first phase of the investigated period. Now, their support for positive images had vanished as well. Statements from politicians made up 11 percent of all negative statements on military women. Half of these came from the Pentagon, the other half from Republican Congress members. Democrats from both houses and Senators from both parties—the former supporters of integration—were no longer represented in debates. This reflects shifts in power relations in Congress and power gains for Republicans aiming to reverse the Clinton administration's modernization of military gender relations. Without a Congressional majority and in the absence of major military interventions, Democrats were unable (and probably unwilling) to engage in pro-integration discourses in the media.

Since the early 1990s, interest groups against integration had been established and were participating actively in the debate. It is likely that parts of the military outsourced anti-women campaigns to civilian organizations and lobbyists. Since civil society representatives were rather strongly represented in the examined media—in 30 percent of all statements—and the negative majority among their statements had become even more prevalent (76 percent), this group contributed even more strongly to negative trends than before. They were also the only group to grow, thus diminishing the representation of all others. Fifty-four percent of their statements argued against integration, 22 percent depicted military women negatively. Military effectiveness and sexual violence were the most frequent arguments, contributing strongly to the "sexualization" of debates. Civil society contributed 15 percent to positive statements on military women, 31 percent to positive ones on integration, 36 percent to negative ones on military women, and a majority of 55 percent to negative ones on integration. In only 9 percent of their statements military women were portrayed favorably, with professionalism being the most important category, and in only 15 percent integration was supported, most often through efficiency arguments.

Significant changes also occurred within the military's statements, which accounted for 10 percent of all statements. This group was the only one with a positive majority of about three quarters. All of their statements were on integration: Among positive ones in this category, they accounted for 33 percent, among negative ones for 6 percent. Military women received no evaluations at all. Since the general discourse increasingly shifted from military women to the process of integration, arguments no longer referred to achievements and contributions, but to institutional perspectives. Equality was strongly revalued and accounted for 42 percent of positive statements on integration. Even the military no longer gave priority to efficiency arguments. Now, statements from the Army made up the vast majority (83 percent). The rest was distributed equally across the other services. The positive majority in the military's statements was, however, unable to turn the general trend around. The omission of positive statements by politicians and the increase in negative statements by civil society organizations could not be counterbalanced.

The dominantly positive military statements reflect inner-military discourses. The RAND Corporation report (Harrell and Miller 1997) that the Pentagon had commissioned showed that acceptance of integration was on average relatively high within the military in this second phase of the investigated time period. Service members considered the impact of integration on readiness, cohesion, and morale to be low. They also evaluated leadership qualities and qualifications as being more influential than gender, and women's performance was assessed as equal to that of men. Lines of conflict within units ran more often along occupations or ranks than sexes. The majority supported relaxing combat exclusions and gender-integrated training. The more women were in leadership positions, the more content units were with the integration process. Within forces with a higher proportion of ground combat troops, particularly the Army and the Marines, men tended to favor the retention of current regulations. Hostility towards women and integration was mostly expressed by men of lower rank, who felt especially underprivileged in the course of modernization processes. This differentiation in attitudes was also found in reporting: Most official representatives of the military expressed positive attitudes towards integration, but those parts of the military that had lost prestige and influence in restructuring processes were more frequently negative.

Summarizing this second phase of the examined period, we can conclude that the functions of gender ideologies in media discourses had changed under the new strategic and political conditions. No military intervention fostered public support for military women or the need to supply positive images in war propaganda and media spectacles. Political support declined due to changed power relations in the legislative. Recruitment requirements and an increasingly competitive military job market made the military less dependent on female labor. Increased integration was blamed for downsizing and for other negative effects of military reform. Anti-integration sentiments and negative representations were revalued as a strategy to criticize modernization processes, which were interpreted as "trivializing," "civilizing," "deheroizing," and consequently as a "demasculinization" of the military and of warfare. These discourses reflected a loss of prestige and power of traditional military elites and increased job cutbacks.

In the absence of larger military interventions, the media's interest in military gender issues declined or shifted to the scandalizing of "sexual misconduct" within the services. Supporters of integration from different realms of society contributed less to debates, and opponents were able to gain discursive hegemony. Integration debates became a matter of cultural values and not of military efficiency. Under these conditions, discourses were remasculinized. This was also mirrored in recruitment campaigns which again increasingly focused on traditional "male" characteristics (Brown 2006). The Army did not feature women as often as it had before, and the Navy also increasingly focused on adventure and war-prone masculinity. The Marines continued putting forward elitism and masculinism. In the media, opponents of integration constructed women's exclusion as an anti-modernist value orientation. Arguments from the realm of sexual morals were increasingly utilized to argue women's unsuitability for military service. Sexual violence was depicted as a natural effect of a masculine warrior ethos, implicitly blaming women for the increasing problem of sexual abuse. Clinging to traditional, irrational gender stereotypes was supposed to offer protection from modernization processes. Gender differences were essentialized and constructed as the main frame through which social order was perceived. Comparability of racial and gender integration was thus denied. In opposition to the convergence of civilian and military occupations and the loss of relevance of traditional masculinity in warfare, nostalgic images of lost warrior masculinity were fostered. Military women were excluded from this warrior ethos: they allegedly served only out of egoistic, pragmatic, or career-related reasons. "True" women would reject serving in combat positions and ordinary female soldiers were merely pressured to say otherwise by career women in officer ranks.

Patriotic heroines in the "War on Terror" (phase 3: 2000–2005)

In the last phase of the examined period, trends towards differentiation of military masculinity and femininity ideologies were continued. The main context for these developments was the "War on Terror" and its influence on recruitment conditions. Flexible assignment and deployment of female personnel became increasingly important. In the course of strategic reform, units were redefined as combat troops which suffered from a lack of male personnel; the need to co-locate support with combat troops brought many women into high-risk positions. The strategic imperatives of the intervention and the tense recruitment situation raised the dependency on the female workforce. In this context, reporting on military gender issues increased again and was again overwhelmingly positive in content. Strategic and political conditions during the "War on Terror," however, had ambivalent effects on gender integration and associated ideologies. Males-only ground combat troops and male-dominated private military companies (PMCs) gained in strategic importance. Neoconservative hegemony in the political realm impeded gender equality measures inside and outside the military. Though reporting approximated some of the patterns observed during the Persian Gulf War, the different political and strategic contexts caused some crucial differences in media gender ideologies.

Recruitment during the "War on Terror"

This third phase of the examined 1990–2005 period was characterized by a difficult recruitment situation. One reason was the growing economy, which until 2001 led to the lowest civilian unemployment rate since the establishment of the AVF (Warner/Asch 2001: 170). New recruitment shortages began already in 1998. From 1998/99 on, the military needed 10 percent of the cohort of 18- to 24-year-old men to sustain force size. This was a difficult goal under the conditions of a robust civilian economy. Too few officers could be retained in service, and for communication, information technology, cryptology, and machine maintenance too few enlisted personnel were available (ibid.: 180). Recruitment shortages also negatively affected the quality of personnel. The proportion of high-quality recruits had been sinking since the late 1990s. While it was 74.4 percent of new recruits in 1992, it fell to only 59.1 percent in 1999. The strong civilian economy reduced higher qualified recruits by 15,000 a year, because more young people were choosing to go to college (ibid.: 184f.). The percentage of recruits in the lowest qualification categories was simultaneously rising (Armor and Gilroy 2007: 10). Since the Army had reduced troops the most, it faced the highest personnel demands. It had trouble meeting its recruitment goals already in 1997. As a consequence it increased its resources for recruitment and doubled the permissible numbers of recruits without high-school degrees. Educational benefits such as the Army College Fund were widened (Asch *et al.* 2001: 10). The Navy and the Air Force were also struggling with shortages (ibid.: xii). To increase the propensity to enlist and retention rates, military wages were raised by 4.8 percent in 2000 (Warner and Asch 2001: 181); resources for recruitment were drastically enhanced (ibid.: 185). A report on recruitment problems was commissioned to the RAND-Corporation. To improve the situation, it recommended counterbalancing the lack of high-quality male recruits by admitting more women (Asch *et al.* 2001: xiii).

In addition to these general developments, the military's growth in context of the "War on Terror" put substantial pressure on recruitment (Armor/Gilroy 2007: 1). The military budget was expanded and was 25 percent higher in real terms than at the height of the Vietnam War in 1968 (Avant and Sigelman 2009: 34). Though unemployment began to rise again after 2001 and youth populations had been growing since 1996 (ibid.: 11), the war countervailed these favorable recruitment conditions. After 9/11, enlistment sharply declined, as had been the case during the Persian Gulf War in 1991. This particularly concerned African-American enlistment rates, which had experienced a downward trend ever since that war and reached new lows (ibid.: 4). Increased personnel demands raised female representation to about 15 percent of the 1.4 million regular troops (Table 3.1), supplemented by about 150,000 female reservists (Gabbert 2007: 33). These demands also led women of lower rank to be sent to the frontline and more female reservists to be assigned to duty (Williams 2005: 98). Women accounted for 14 percent of both Army and of Navy personnel, 19.5 percent of Air Force personnel, and 6 percent of the Marines (Brown 2006: 2). Their proportions among enlisted and officer ranks were about equal. In all services, over 90 percent of occupations were open to women, while the proportion of actually available jobs remained limited by combat exclusions. Only 70 percent of Army, 62 percent of Marines, 91 percent of Navy, and 99 percent of Air Force jobs were open (Segal/Segal 2004: 28). Women were still overrepresented in traditional occupations, but less so than during the 1990s: 55 percent served in health care and in administration (ibid.: 29). Their representation in non-traditional fields such as engineering, machine maintenance, tactical operations, supply and provisioning increased. So did their proportion at higher ranks (Williams 2005: 98).

Beyond these shifts, strategic reform had contradicting effects on women's roles and status: first, by revaluing ground combat and Special Forces (and thus units from which women were largely excluded), and second, by increasing the necessity for flexible regular troops, which required relaxing combat exclusion regulations. The "War on Terror" and especially the intervention in Iraq heightened pressure on ground combat troops, which affected the Army the most. To meet flexibility requirements, the Army was reconfigured into a lighter and faster force. Combat brigades were redefined as "self-contained units of action." These train and serve together with their support troops, the so-called Forward Support Companies (FSCs), in which many women serve (Shanker 2005). With these redefinitions, women's service became problematic due to the collocation rule which forbids the assignment of women to units that are stationed together with combat troops. Problems also arose in reconnaissance units, which had not been defined as combat troops when they were established and developed, but now became part of the Army's fast-deploying combat troops. As a result, the Army had to dismiss women from these units in 2002 (WREI n.d.). Flexible assignment and deployment of female troops thus became a crucial consideration; in this context, combat exclusion laws were dysfunctional because they inhibited the efficient utilization of large contingents of personnel. The Army circumvented formal limitations by redefining women's status within the FSCs and thereby prevented their dismissal. In an internal document, the Army even planned to relax the collocation rule in 2004 (Murnane 2007: 1094). The dependency on female personnel in the Iraq intervention enabled service even in areas affected by exclusionary policies (Titunik 2008: 162).

Another gender-related consequence of strategic reform and increasing flexibility of warfare was the rising importance of private security and military companies. When the US officially defeated Iraqi forces in 2003, one out of ten deployed Americans was a private contractor. The first statistics of the Pentagon to become publicly available counted 100,000 private contractors and 133,000 regular troops in Iraq in 2006. A 2008 Congress report spoke of 190,000 contractors, which would exceed the numbers of regular troops. A total of 30,000 to 35,000 of these contractors served in combat positions. Since 2003, the US government has spent 86 billion dollars on the outsourcing of military tasks to private companies. The infamous Blackwater company, later renamed Xe Services, is only one of 300 companies serving in Iraq. Employees of PMCs were also among the troops involved in the Abu Ghraib torture scandal (Avant and Sigelman 2009: 4ff.).

Higate (2009, 4) identifies the privatization of military tasks as a "key moment of (re)masculinization in the contemporary period". The ranks of PMCs are often filled with ex-military staff who lost their jobs during downsizing and couldn't make use of their military training on civilian labor markets. The losers of modernization processes thus became the winners of the privatization of warfare. These tendencies are related to larger developments in the world economy that affected the state-military relationship and promoted exchange between state and private military labor markets:

> [D]ominance of post-Cold War free markets ... have fuelled a strong tendency to outsource traditional government functions. ... [N]ational militaries have been downsized, thereby providing a large number of (mainly) men trained in "legitimate discharge of violence" ripe for recruitment by well-paying PMSCs [Private Military and Security Companies].
>
> (ibid.: 5)

PMCs are not bound to national borders and recruit from all over the world. They employ a significant number of female personnel, but also assign men from third world countries such as Bangladesh, Nepal, or the Philippines to traditionally "female" tasks in support (ibid.: 13ff.). Former resistance fighters from Fiji, Uganda, or Latin America are assigned the riskier tasks in combat (Schultz and Yeung 2005). Labor division is thus not only gendered, but also ethnically and nationally categorized, with the "inferior" work assigned to those from the global periphery. On privatized security markets, richer countries recruit from poorer regions that offer cheaper labor. Service in private security and military companies becomes an important source of revenue for the countries providing this workforce.

The privatization of warfare also has the advantage of reducing the number of official casualties: mercenaries who are killed in action do not appear in national statistics (Higate 2009: 11).

The relationship between state and war is also altered by this privatizing of military tasks, which are increasingly controlled by the market (not by the state). As a consequence, privatization negatively influences transparency and democratic control (Avant and Sigelman 2009: 2). Since the executive branch concludes contracts with PMCs, its control over military policy is enhanced and Congress' influence weakened. The president can raise the number of private forces without authorization from Congress and without political debate. Congress' attempts to widen its influence on PMCs was repelled by President Bush Junior (ibid.: 16f.). It has little access to private businesses and cannot acquire information on internal structures of companies, directives for promotion, or qualification requirements (ibid.: 12ff.). Until recently, the government did not even provide data on the deployment of PMCs. Information is still not centrally available and hence less accessible. Private companies are also allowed to retain certain information to secure fair business competition. As a consequence, there is no regular media reporting on PMCs, severely limiting access to information on the actual human costs of the war (ibid.: 19ff.).

Despite revaluation of ground combat and increasing privatization of warfare, the legal status of women did not change significantly in the regular forces during the early years of the twenty-first century. Integration, however, was viewed critically by powerful civilian interest groups, which reinforced remasculinizing tendencies on the political level and countered the trend towards liberalization of combat exclusion. The religious right, which had already expanded its influence during the Reagan and Bush Senior administrations, became a key player in the fierce resistance against women's military integration. This group provided the basis for the success of Bush Junior (Gabbert 2007: 124). Anti-feminist policies shaped his presidency, not only in regard to the military. His administration abolished, impeded, or strongly reduced the influence of institutions and committees that had been introduced to support and protect women's interests. Highly visible positions of power were filled with anti-feminists, and reproductive rights were strongly curtailed (Finlay 2006). Parts of the neoconservative elites were dedicated to repressing the "feminization" of the Armed Forces. Visible participants in the debates were lobbyists such as Elaine Donnelly and her right-wing conservative think tank *Center for Military Readiness,* along with representatives of the influential *Heritage Foundation*, which supports neo-liberal economic policy, preventive military strikes, and conservative family values. In cooperation with Republican representatives within the House Armed Services Committee, they worked towards legally prohibiting women's assignment to FSCs. In the face of recruitment shortages, this legislature was, however, successfully opposed by Army, Pentagon, and representatives from both parties (Titunik 2008: 163).

While military personnel policy did not conform to conservative values in this case, the political context provided more opportunities for opponents of integration to enforce their interests. Their main successes were twofold: first, the competence of DACOWITS, military women's main advocate, was severely cut. The Pentagon let its charter run out in 2002, reduced its membership by half, and redefined its mission: Gender equality and integration were removed as main responsibilities and replaced by the improvement of readiness and family issues (WREI n.d.). Second, opponents successfully introduced new regulations requiring the military to seek Congressional approval for any changes in personnel policies affecting gender integration. The National Defense Authorization Act for 2006 was amended so that the combat exclusion rules introduced in 1994 were upgraded to the status of a law. The objective of expanding women's roles and inhibiting the closure of occupations no longer received mention in the military budget. While women could remain within the FSCs, the Pentagon is now required to inform Congress in the future before ground combat rules are changed or positions can be opened or closed to women (Murnane 2007: 1094). For the first time since the foundation of the AVF, female participation declined after 2003 (Table 3.1). Legal changes overthrew the consensus on the goal of furthering integration, cemented remaining exclusions, and made further steps dependent on future political power relations. Congress was able to gain control over female participation in the regular troops, while it effectively lost influence on the primarily male forces of PMCs.

Gender ideologies in integration debates

Due to the ongoing intervention, reporting on military gender issues increased again during this last, third period examined (Table 4.6). About one third of the analyzed articles appeared in this phase, most being published in 2003 and 2005. Between 2000 and 2002, only sporadic articles dealt with women in the military; they were no longer considered newsworthy per se (Hanson 2002: 4). Even the intervention in Afghanistan failed to increase reporting on military gender issues, though gender stereotypes were extensively instru-mentalized to legitimize military engagement in the region (Tickner 2002; O'Connor 2002; Young 2003). Unlike during the Persian Gulf War and the "War on Terror" in Iraq, images of oppressed Muslim women were infre-quently presented in opposition to emancipated US military women. Only the personnel and strategic problems during the Iraq invasion again raised interest in military gender issues. Almost half of all analyzed articles between 2000 and 2005 were on women serving in this mission. As during the Persian Gulf War, many of these articles dealt with women casualties and POWs. Two articles on the Abu Ghraib torture scandal addressed gender integration. The second most frequent issue was debates on exclusions, which also directly related to the ongoing intervention in most cases. Most of the reporting on gender issues was thus initiated by the war in Iraq. Recruitment shortages and war pro-paganda brought military gender issues back into media focus, reflecting the functionality of images of military women for both domestic and foreign policy debates.

Table 4.6 Distribution across newspapers, genres, and time (phase 3)

	The New York Times				The Washington Post				Total
	Reports	Features	Editorials	Total	Reports	Features	Editorials	Total	
2000	0	0	0	0	1	0	0	1	1
2001	0	0	0	0	0	0	2	2	2
2002	0	0	0	0	0	1	0	1	1
2003	1	1	2	4	0	1	4	5	9
2004	0	0	0	0	0	3	1	4	4
2005	1	2	1	4	4	3	2	9	13
Total	2	3	3	8	5	8	9	22	30

Overall, depictions of military women and their integration were overwhelmingly positive. The relation between positive and negative statements was once again reversed and approximated the ratio of the early 1990s (Table 4.7). The positive majority was, however, somewhat less overwhelming than originally, i.e. 66 versus 71 percent. Again, military women, and not the process of integration, were the focus of reporting. Positive statements on female service members accounted for 37 percent of all statements and were thus the largest category. The second largest were positive statements on integration (29 percent). Twenty-four percent referred negatively to military women, only 10 percent to integration. The formerly smallest category (positive statements on military women) had become the largest again, and the formerly largest (negative statements on integration) the smallest. The relationship between different statement categories from the early 1990s was thus re-established. War had again moved military women to the center-stage of media attention and affected the content of their representations positively.

Like in the previous phase, the number of articles in the two newspapers differed (Table 4.6). This time the WP produced almost three times as many articles as the NYT. However, the number of statements was less unequal: Due to the NYT's longer articles, statements from the WP constituted only a thin majority of 56 percent. The intensity of reporting was therefore more equal than the total numbers of articles suggest. The relation between positive and negative statements in both newspapers approximated overall ratios between positive and negative categories. Positive statements were slightly underrepresented in the NYT at 63 percent and slightly overrepresented in the WP at 68 percent, compared to the ratio of positive statements in overall reporting (66 percent). The positive-negative ratio within the different genres was also comparable to the overall results.

Table 4.7 Distribution of positive and negative statements (phase 3)

	Positive statements	Negative statements	Total
Military Women	37%	24%	61%
Integration	29%	10%	39%
Total	66%	34%	100%

Positive statements were slightly overrepresented in reports and features and slightly underrepresented in editorials. The former two genres dominated reporting in the WP, while reporting was equally distributed across genres in the NYT. Comparing results to the first two phases of the examined period reveals that a stronger (positive) consensus prevails in war time.

Under the strategic conditions and political power relations of this period, the positive trend in reporting was not as prevalent as it had been in the early 1990s, and the content of positive depictions had changed. Conservative hegemony was expressed in more "patriotic" depictions of military women. In the context of the "War on Terror," they were increasingly portrayed as dedicated patriots, and integration was more frequently legitimized as a patriotic measure. For the first time, patriotism and heroism became the primary modes of representation, overtaking professionalism and competence. Nineteen percent of positive statements on military women portrayed them as patriotic and heroic, while professionalism only featured in 11 percent and ranked behind courage at 14 percent and emancipation at 12 percent. In 10 percent of statements within this category, women appeared as tough and resilient. Another 10 percent percent claimed that they were already serving on the frontlines and deserved credit for it. Even the formerly insignificant depiction of women as reliable comrades reached 10 percent. This was likely an effect of debates on women's assignment to ground combat support units, which was supported by most military and political representatives. The smallest statement categories were those on women as responsible military leaders (3 percent), women wanting to take part in combat (4 percent), and mothers as competent soldiers (4 percent). The perspective of the involved female soldiers was no longer featured in argumentations. Neither were the opinions of military men or military husbands. Public opinion remained an important point of reference only in contra-argumentations. Discourses in favor of integration had thus become less "democratic" and the revaluation of family values decreased statements defending the compatibility of motherhood and military service.

Within positive statements on integration, the distribution was unequal across argumentative strategies, showing a preference for effectiveness arguments. Like in the early 1990s, exclusion was argued as being inefficient in the greatest relative proportion of statements (34 percent). At the same time, equality (20 percent) and patriotism (15 percent) also represented influential arguments. Ten percent of statements argued against the "protective myth" and another 10 percent claimed the gender-neutrality of war. The performance principle—a main point of reference for the corporate image of the neo-liberal military during the early 1990s—no longer played a major role. Neither did refutation of outdated values and the attitudes of the general public. These three accounted for only 3 percent of positive statements on integration each. Though this quantitative distribution shows some similarity to that of the early 1990s, a closer reading reveals that the contents of many statement categories had shifted in a way not mirrored in the relative proportion of statement groups. Kelly Oliver (2007) has shown how women and their bodies have been perceived and depicted as powerful weapons in the Afghanistan and Iraq wars by the media and the administration. These discursive patterns were also observed in the media examined here. Argumentative strategies regarding effectiveness and efficiency had particularly changed. These referred less to qualifications of women and more to the instrumentalization of traditional gender stereotypes in warfare and the strategic disadvantage that exclusion would represent in the "War on Terror." Women's discrimination was constructed as a contradiction to the objectives of the war. The image of the gender-neutral female soldier became more martial: Not technology neutralized gender, but courage and heroism. Pragmatic career orientation of military women was no longer associated with professionalism, but mourned as a (necessary) loss of femininity.

The increased importance of traditional gender ideals was also reflected in contra-arguments. Overall, traditional images of a naturally weaker sex in need of protection provided the basis for most arguments in negative categories. Among negative statements on military women, which were twice as frequent as negative ones on integration, arguments concerning their mental instability were most prevalent, as had been the case in the early 1990s. These statements, which portrayed women as fearful, instable, and childlike, accounted for 32 percent in this category. The second largest group of arguments concerned incompatibility of motherhood and military service (17 percent). Ten percent depicted women as physically inadequate and highlighted their bodily weakness and lack of endurance. Eight percent depicted them as masculinized and 7 percent as foreign and lost in the male world of the military. Four percent of statements each claimed that women did not want to serve in combat or took advantage of their male comrades. Men's negative attitudes towards integration were mentioned equally frequently. Depictions of women as "beautiful souls" included misogynist prejudice which implied that women could sustain their peacefulness and virtuousness only if they were kept in appropriate "female spheres." If they entered male spaces, such as the military, they were potentially more aggressive than men. This was most obvious in depictions that mentioned exceptional cruelty as a characteristic of military women. Due to the Abu Ghraib torture scandal this category appeared in 13 percent of negative statements on military women. Negative statements on integration were distributed across only a small number of categories. For the first time, military effectiveness was not the most frequent argument and reached only 28 percent within this category. Thirty-one percent featured protection as the main rationale for exclusion and 28 percent the public's opposition against integration. Thirteen percent claimed that exclusion represented a central US value and should thus be upheld, even if it contradicted pragmatic considerations.

Positive trends were supported by almost all groups of actors participating in media debates. Journalists' statements, which were again strongly overrepresented (72 percent), were again overwhelmingly on the side of supporters of integration. Nonetheless, the overrepresentation of positive statements was lower than in the early 1990s when they had accounted for 81 percent of journalists' statements. Following an established pattern, positive depictions of military women were the most frequent group, accounting for 43 percent of their statements. Of these, 22 percent were portrayals of patriotic and heroic military women, 14 percent depictions of them as emancipated, 11 percent each as courageous and professional, and 10 percent as resilient. Another 10 percent claimed that women were already serving in combat. Journalists contributed an overwhelming proportion to positive statements on military women, namely 83 percent. The situation was somewhat different for positive statements on integration, among which journalists accounted for only 61 percent and which made up only 24 percent of their statements. Within this category, efficiency arguments prevailed at 31 percent over patriotism and gender-neutrality of war (15 percent each) as well as equality and refutation of the protection argument (13 percent each).

Due to the dominance of their statements, journalists were also strongly represented among negative statements on military women (75 percent). Twenty-four percent of their statements belonged in this category within which mental weakness featured in 37 percent of statements. The rest of negative depictions accounted for between 6 percent and 11 percent, with motherhood and the threat of masculinization as most frequent argumentations. Only 8 percent of journalists' statements belonged to the category of negative statements on integration. They still accounted for 56 percent of total statements in this category. Half of these referred to the lack of public acceptance.

The military and politicians were also overwhelmingly positive, but contributed less often to debates. The military, whose statements were 80 percent positive, accounted for only 7 percent of all statements. Military representatives contributed 6 percent to positive statements on military women and 10 percent to positive ones on integration. Most of these came from the Army; the remainder was distributed equally across the Navy and Air Force. No statements came from the Marines. The distribution across different arguments was relatively equal. Only military effectiveness was mentioned more frequently. The 20 percent of negative statements was distributed equally between Navy and Air Force. The rationales for exclusion were mental weakness, female cruelty, and the protection of women. The military contributed little to negative categories: 3 percent to negative statements on women and 6 percent to those on integration. The Army had the most to lose from the enforcement of combat exclusions and was consequently the most positive group. Overall positive trends in the military's attitudes towards women were also mirrored in recruitment campaigns. These supported the dissolution of the masculinist image of the Armed Forces by placing their TV spots during shows such as *Friends* to reach broader audiences (Brown 2006: 15).

An even more positive group was politicians, who contributed 10 percent of statements. The trends in their evaluations of military gender issues had again completely switched, this time from a 100 percent negative attitude in the late 1990s to 85 percent positive after 2000. A majority (61 percent) referred positively to integration and 24 percent depicted military women positively. Half of these statements came from Democratic members of Congress, one quarter from Republican representatives. The remaining quarter was made up by Pentagon representatives and to a lesser extent by Republican senators. Democratic senators did not participate in debates. About one third of politicians' statements legitimized integration as an equality measure, with no significant difference between both parties. Military effectiveness and patriotism were also popular points of reference. While only contributing 7 percent to positive statements on military women, politicians supported positive trends in evaluations of integration by contributing 23 percent to this category. Only 15 percent of politicians' statements were negative, with all of these referring to integration and none to military women. Thereby, they contributed 16 percent to negative statements on integration, which all came from Republican representatives. Military effectiveness, US values, lack of public support, and necessary protection of women were the main arguments. The distribution of arguments across actors and the content of argumentations mirror the attempts of parts of the Republican Party to prevent further integration and enforce traditional gender ideals, but also a broad pro-integration consensus among both parties in the context of the war effort.

The overall positive trends among military and political representatives were counterbalanced by the contributions of civil society. The Christian right and neoconservative activists were intensely engaged within this sector. At 10 percent, this group of actors was equally represented as the military and politicians, but it was the only group whose statements were negative by a large majority (72 percent). Fifty percent of civil society's statements referred negatively to military women and 22 percent to integration. Among the first category, motherhood was their most frequent argument, followed by physical inadequacy and female cruelty. Military effectiveness and protection of women were their main arguments against integration. Their argumentative strategies were based on traditional gender ideologies and concentrated on normative and cultural dimensions. Civil society contributed 22 percent to both negative categories. Their positive statements were equally distributed between statements on military women and integration (both 14 percent of civil society's statements), contributing 3 percent to overall statements in the former and 6 percent in the latter category.

Gendering of war

Traditional gender stereotypes attained new functions in media representations of the "War on Terror," which provided the main discursive context for debates on military gender issues. They were utilized to legitimize the intervention by showcasing victimized Muslim women waiting to be freed by US forces (Sjoberg and Gentry 2008; Masters 2009):

> Burqa-clad women were featured on the cover of the *New York Times* magazine (in a feature story that, interestingly enough, had absolutely nothing to say about women), as well as *Business Week, Newsweek, Time* and other general interest magazines. ... [T]he issue had been barely covered by the mainstream media or even publicly discussed by policy makers in the past.
> (Stabile and Kumar 2005: 765)

The defeat of the Taliban was consequently illustrated by images of Afghan women freed by progressive Western males (ibid.: 773). These images not only functioned as a gendered tool of war propaganda, but also as an Orientalist discourse constructing an opposition between backward Muslim and emancipated Western women. This dualism helped deny anti-feminist tendencies in the West:

> This logic not only erases the struggles of women in Afghanistan for their own liberation, but it also erases the struggles of women in the West against sexism. By presenting women's equality as a natural part of "Western humanist values," centuries of women's political activity for suffrage (gained less than a century ago), for equal pay (still not achieved today), for reproductive rights (presently under attack by Christian fundamentalist terrorists), are evacuated from history.
>
> (ibid.: 775)

This discourse was also prevalent in debates on military gender issues during the Iraq intervention. Emancipated military women and gender integration were used as a proof of US superiority and progressiveness and as coherent with the alleged motivations for the war.

Traditional gender ideologies were also instrumentalized in media reporting on events during the war. The narratives on the two US soldiers Jessica Lynch and Lynndie England were particularly gendered (Stachowitsch 2008). Despite the obvious differences in the content of both media events, they had certain elements in common: both deflected public attention from political and military contexts to individual soldiers in a critical phase of the war, and both used gender ideologies in the process. Personalizing and depoliticizing narrative strategies have played an important role in US representations of war since the Vietnam War. Their main purpose is to redirect attention from the system onto individuals. By doing so, war seems less a national than a personal experience without historical or political backgrounds. It thus becomes harder to criticize ongoing interventions or the political leadership (Jeffords 1996: 226). Political contexts are concealed by a "politics of spectacle" which highlights the opposition of good and evil in scandalizing discourses (Kellner 2003). Since narratives of war also construct notions of masculinity and femininity and reflect changes in gender relations (Jeffords 1996: 228f.), processes of personalization are also always of a gendered nature.

In the case of Private Jessica Lynch, the government, military, and media constructed a story about a patriotic heroine rescued by courageous US forces. Lynch was taken captive by Iraqi forces when her unit was ambushed in March 2003. The media claimed that she had fought fiercely and had been shot and stabbed various times. Special Operation Forces came to her rescue and stormed the hospital in which Lynch was kept, accompanied by a camera team. Images of the tired, but thankful rescued soldier, draped with an American flag, went around the world. Despite dubious sources, this heroic story became the official version. Back home, Lynch was welcomed by parades and decorations. Only after the British newspaper *The Guardian* had published a detailed deconstruction of the narrative, the US press also began to question the spin on Lynch's story. It turned out that she had not fired her gun at all, because it had jammed (Chinni 2003). She had faced no danger at the hands of her captors and was treated for her injuries at the hospital, which had been completely unguarded at the time of the Special Forces arrival. It thus became clear that the mass media had offered themselves to the government and the military as effective propaganda tools.

Lynch's story was used to mobilize support for the much criticized intervention. Gendered narratives and stereotypes played a major role in it. Contradictory discourses represented her as both a child-like victim and a courageous fighter. In both roles, her own agency was denied: "Everybody felt like she was their adopted child" (Associated Press 2003b, Fox News Online). Her fate seemed dependent on male actors: first the Iraqi forces, later the doctors, and last the US Special Forces. The latter appeared as the embodiment of military masculinity ideals, destined to save the "damsel in distress" (Goff 2003). Even fighting women were thus depicted as objects of male protection:

> On her hospital bed Pfc. Jessica Lynch peered out from the sheet with which she'd been covering her head in fear. . . . Jessica held up her hand and grabbed the Ranger doctor's hand, and held onto it for the entire time and said, "Please don't let anybody leave me." It was clear she . . . didn't want to be left anywhere near the enemy.
>
> (Associated Press 2003a, Fox News Online)

Lynch's status as a victim was supported by reports which claimed that she had been raped by her captors (Colford/Siemasko 2003, *New York Daily News*). Though these claims have never been verified, the imagined cruelty of the enemy and notions of patriarchal protectionism were used to help legitimize the preemptive invasion of Iraq (Goff 2003). At the same time, the media spectacle became an important point of reference in debates on integration. Supporters presented the story as proof that women could serve heroically. Opponents used it as evidence that it was morally and strategically wrong to put women in frontline positions, especially after it became known that the story about her resistance had been a propaganda spin. The alleged rape was also used to argue for women's exclusion and highlight their unsuitability for military service. Feminists were accused of circulating false information on Lynch's captivity to weaken restrictions on military participation. Lynch was insulted as an opportunist whose fame was undeserved and took credit away from more courageous male soldiers, who had actually died for their country (Goff 2003). These constructions of women's selfish motivations were also a common image in general reporting on military gender integration. Historical patterns of such slander by doubting their morals and integrity (Seifert 1988) were also applied to Lynch's story. Rumors were spread that she had posed naked for photographs with male colleagues in military barracks (Rush 2003, *New York Daily News*). These reports were also never confirmed. Lynch's image thus acquired multiple functions for different political, military, and social groups. Their interests in the war effort and in integration debates determined how favorably she was portrayed.

Another strongly gendered media event of the "War on Terror" was the Abu Ghraib torture scandal. A group of male and female US service members had systematically tortured and sexually abused Iraqi prisoners to "soften them up" for interrogations. The abuse had been extensively photographed. One of the most widely discussed images featured Private Lynndie England, as she was holding a naked male prisoner on a leash. Internal military investigations into these events became public in April 2004. These identified four male and three female members of the military police and one male member of military intelligence as the main perpetrators. Private England attracted most media attention, even after a male soldier had been convicted as the "ringleader" of the abuse. Media reports called her a "symbol" of the abuse (Fisher 2004, WP: B01; Stevenson 2004, NYT: 4/2), the "most public face of the scandal" (Zernike 2004, NYT: 1/1; Reuters 2004, NYT: A8), "central figure" (Associated Press 2004, NYT: A8), and "synonymous with the abuse" (Davenport and Amon 2004, WP: A18). She was later convicted of conspiracy, abuse of prisoners, and "indecent acts" and sentenced to three years in prison.

Like the Lynch case, the media spectacle of the Abu Ghraib scandal was individualized and gendered. Media discourses processed the scandal by constructing the involved soldiers, and especially Lynndie England, as aberrations from "natural" gender roles and from military masculinity ideals. The outrageousness of England's behavior was pointed out frequently. Historical patterns of depicting violent women supported these narrative strategies. The specific newsworthiness of women as perpetrators of violence is explained by the hegemonic image of female peacefulness, which makes female aggression seem even more scandalous, excessive, and deviant than that of men. The violations of human rights at Abu Ghraib were thus concealed by scandalized female cruelty (Harders 2004: 1108). The role of the male soldiers involved received less media attention and was rationalized as "normal" male behavior:

> [The subsequent courts-martial] reified power in the hands of the mostly male soldiers at Abu Ghraib who acted in stereotypically masculine ways, e.g. punching, beating, and forcing others to be humiliated. Such abuse was rationalized in instrumental terms as punishment, interrogation, and softening-up prisoners.
>
> (Caldwell and Mestrovic 2008: 295)

This kind of gendering helped shift responsibility from government and military authorities onto a few "black sheep." Criticism of Secretary of Defense Donald Rumsfeld and the Bush administration was thereby absorbed. With this strategy, attention was also deflected from the role of PMCs in Iraq and from the 27 employees of the firm CACI, which had been responsible for interrogation at Abu Ghraib prison. In the context of privatization of warfare, women were apparently assigned new military tasks, such as sexual torture to gather intelligence.

In the NYT and the WP, very few articles related Abu Ghraib or Jessica Lynch's story directly to gender issues. Neither captivity of military women, nor female involvement in torture led to substantial criticism of integration. Even in these more liberal newspapers, however, the misogynist discourses in other media were hardly criticized, and activists fighting for the re-establishment of exclusions, such as Elaine Donnelly and Phyllis Schlafly, could claim a larger role in debates and were cited more often than feminist activists and supporters of integration.

The content of reporting was gendered. Features particularly relied on images of heroic men, proud military wives, and deviant male and female villains. Male and female soldiers involved in the torture were depicted as aberrations from the ideal type of military masculinity defined by discipline, honor, and courage. England was often juxtaposed to the "good" military man, embodied by reservist Joseph Darby, who had informed his superiors of the goings-on at Abu Ghraib. The WP, in particular, published detailed features on Darby as a typical American hero with the right motivation for service. He was cited as saying: "It's not what I went over there for" (Williamson 2004c, WP: A12) and: "It was just wrong. I knew I had to do something" (Higham/Stephens 2004, WP: A01). He was portrayed as a patriot and a Christian, who had gone to Iraq with "his knapsack filled with pocket Bibles and toys" (ibid.). These characterizations of Darby as a disciplined, responsible soldier were connected to depictions of his idyllic family life, in which his proud wife played a major role. In the world of the male hero, gender roles were still in order: "They're just a normal family," his sister-in-law was cited as saying in the WP (Williamson 2004b, WP: C04). By presenting England and Darby in opposition to each other, the dichotomy between cruelty and heroism was related to the opposition male/female.

Conservative, right-wing newspapers such as *The Washington Times* (WT) made the scandal a question of gender in more explicit ways. An analysis of the WT's reporting on Abu Ghraib shows that the image of the morally degenerated woman was extensively used to blame women for the scandal. Guilt was extended to all military women, but also to civilian women, feminists, and supporters of integration. The torture scandal was also instrumentalized in integration debates. Uncontrollable sexuality and the possibility of pregnancy—England was pregnant with the child of the main perpetrator of the abuse—were given as reasons to exclude women from the military (Simmons 2004, WT: A21; Scarborough 2004a, WT: A01; Scarborough 2004b, WT: A01; Blanchard 2004, WT: D03). This type of reporting supported claims that integration would hinder military readiness, endanger victory in Iraq, and that it would be unpatriotic and "un-American" to put women in military leadership positions. Insufficient femininity of (military) women was associated with endangering national security. The lobby against integration was given a forum to spread the message that victory was dependent on whether women were allowed to serve. Myths of promiscuity and homosexuality of military women, which had already been propagated during the Second World War to hinder integration (Stiehm 1988: 96), were used to show that England and the other women involved were not "true women." Integration was held responsible for the abuse of Iraqi prisoners, but also for sexual violence against military women:

> What were Congress and the Clinton White House thinking when they began, in earnest, legislative moves that essentially led to the feminization of America's armed forces? Did they think that there would be not cultural implications (pregnancies, rape and sexual assault, etc.)? Did they think there would be no effect on America's military …; scores of reports about women soldiers participating in the mistreatment of male prisoners (including sexual degradation); photographic evidence that the "girls" were equal partners with the "boys" in these criminal acts—during a war, no less; the possibility that one of those "girls," a suspect in these wholly un-American abuses and shameful acts—was impregnated while fighting in a war.
>
> (Simmons 2004, WT: A21)

Military authority and leadership were strongly associated with masculinity, and integration was interpreted as a loss of male power. These patterns have also been observed in Seifert's study of the German Bundeswehr (Seifert 1996), as well as in the general reporting analyzed in the present study. In the coverage of the Abu Ghraib scandal, constructions of women as incompetent military leaders were repeated in the portrayal of Janis Karpinksi, commander of the military police units at the prison. She was depicted as "unmanly" and thus unable to take responsibility:

> Mr. Rumsfeld stood straight up to the world and accepted responsibility for Abu Ghraib. He took it like a man. War is not woman's work. It is man's work—not because men are more brutal or stronger, but because they can endure the stresses of combat and be accountable for the failures those stresses inevitably create. They don't whine, deviously evade, blame others, make up excuses and whimper, "It's not my fault!"
>
> (Wheeler 2004, WT)

Women were accused of cultural insensitivity, and integration was constructed as an affront against the culture of the enemy and thus an impediment to winning the war:

> No values are higher in the Arab world than male honor and female purity. Placing a woman in charge of Iraq prisons when the US was trying to win the hearts and minds of the population was an affront to this culture. … If one is to direct its destinies, one must at least be aware of its cultural myths.
>
> (Devine 2004, WT)

These forms of gendering were also connected to class-related stereotypes. Poor whites often represent an acceptable "other" in US discourses (Gibbons 2004: 8).

By depicting lower social classes as racist and intolerant, middle and upper classes assert their cultural and intellectual superiority (Newitz 1997). Poorer socio-economic groups are often ethnicized in capitalist societies: they are ascribed the role of the primitive in a primitive—civilized dichotomy (ibid.: 134). It is thus morally mandatory to resent them. An inability for social mobility is central in this "white trash" narrative (McCarter 2005).

In this sense, Lynndie England not only represented military women, but also a certain socio-economic group. She was portrayed as a symbol for the lower classes' inability to conform to middle-class gender roles and values. A divorced smoker, pregnant with an illegitimate child, she became the poster girl of deviant "white trash" femininity. An anonymous government representative was even cited as calling her and her family "recycled hillbillies prone to gullability" (Duke 2004, WP: D01). Resentment against lower classes was also expressed in arguments against integration, which accused single mothers of exploiting the welfare system of the military. Elaine Donnelly wrote in a letter to Donald Rumsfeld:

> Overly generous incentives for single parents and large families attract even more unstable, low-income families that depend on the Defense Department's extensive social welfare system. Some feminists have described the military, approvingly, as a "Mecca" for single moms.
>
> (Scarborough 2004a, WT: A01)

Interestingly enough, Jessica Lynch, who was from a very similar background and region as England, was not portrayed in a comparable way. Since her image acquired different functions in war reporting, she was depicted as the ordinary "girl next door," a normal young woman who wanted to be a school teacher and raise a family, but had to join the military out of economic reasons. Joseph Darby was also spared the attribute "white trash." His modest upbringing was not only no obstacle to his heroism, it was also claimed to having inspired it (Williamson 2004a, WP: A16).

The media narratives on Lynch and England express changes in military institutions and in warfare. As in the case of the Somalia intervention, problems of the war in Iraq were interpreted in the context of increased female representation and read through a gendered frame. In Lynch's case, a narrative was constructed in which women were participating in the war, but leadership, authority, and heroism remained reserved for men and coded in masculine terms. Female participation was presented in a way that did not question male supremacy in military matters. In the case of England, the scandal was more bluntly interpreted as a demasculinization of the Armed Forces and the nation. England and other women were held responsible by constructing the scandal as a reversion of "natural" gender roles. Both stories thus ensured the public that men and women were both intensively participating in the "War on Terror," but that they were assigned different functions in the endeavour. Again, these case studies show that the hypothesis of a "positive" trend in reporting during war-time needs to be revised somewhat, i.e. when we consider reporting that does not deal with military gender issues explicitly. Analysis of media outlets other than the moderately liberal NYT and WP also brings to light stronger anti-integration sentiments and anti-feminist notions in discourses on military gender issues. These discursive contexts, as well as political and strategic conditions, are responsible for the differences between reporting during the Persian Gulf War and the "War on Terror." While both events initiated positive trends in media representations, they were different in content and context. The first highlighted the professional soldier in the context of comprehensive equality measures. The second produced more patriotic and traditional images of military women under the conditions of rising conservative resistance against integration.

5 Conclusions

Relations between the material and the cultural

This study has pursued different theoretical and empirical research issues. The main focus lay on the relations between the structural and cultural dimensions of military gender integration. These relations were examined from a political and social science perspective, emphasizing their embeddedness in social, political, and military processes. A materialist research strategy helped to study gender ideologies as adaptations to historically and culturally varying forms of a gender-specific division of labor. In the military context, labor division is determined by technological and strategic conditions, recruitment environments, and legal restrictions on women's service, but also by wider socio-economic processes and political power relations. These multiple factors influence ideology formation, which is always contested by various social groups of actors. These power struggles are carried out—among other spaces—within mass media discourses. The study therefore examined media debates on military gender integration to identify the different functions of gender ideologies. In a discourse-analytical procedure, images of military women and argumentative strategies of opponents and supporters were contextualized within processes of social, military, and political change.

Conclusions on the transformations of gender ideologies and their causes were drawn by comparing different phases of the investigated period from 1990 to 2005 (Figure 5.1). For each of the three phases, the relations between contextual variables and discursive patterns were identified. The focus lay on quantitative and qualitative continuities and discontinuities in argumentation strategies: What were the discursive contents in depictions and arguments? Which functions did they fulfill for opponents and supporters of integration? Which contents were constantly observable? Which changed or disappeared? Under what conditions did changes arise? What were the general effects of integration processes? What were the causes of variations? What were the specific features of each phase? How did different groups of actors participate in debates? The main purpose was to highlight trends and tendencies, not to deduce mechanistic correlations or universally valid causalities. Nonetheless, the results on the relations between structural change and gender ideologies during this period do provide the basis for developing more general hypotheses.

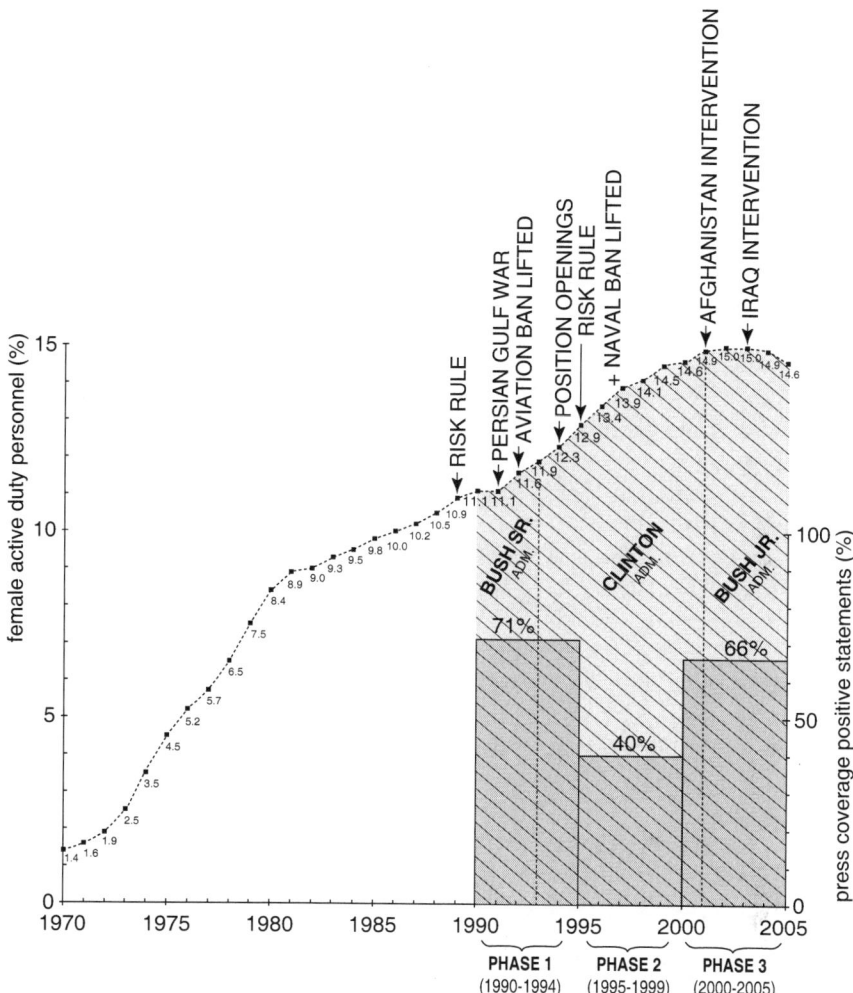

Figure 5.1 Overview of integration process and statement distribution

Structural change in US military and society

The gender-specific division of labor in the military is determined by a set of social, military, and political conditions. Proliferation of technology, professionalization, specialization, and the increased complexity of labor markets are the processes that represent the larger contexts for changes in military gender ideologies. These developments transformed personnel demands and workforce supply, impeded recruitment, and thereby promoted the selective integration of women into military institutions. When warfare had depended on short-term mobilization, the military had required rapid access to large numbers of recruits who would be demobilized shortly after the war. Thus, recruitment was organized by conscription. Technological advances decreased the draft's efficiency because military qualification requirements began to rise above the average education level of young adults (Riche 2005: 23). The introduction of the AVF was not a cause, but already an effect of these developments. Within this framework, civilian occupations in technological, logistic, administrative, and medical support fields gained in relevance (Segal 1995: 764; Warner and Asch 2001: 174): military and civilian work areas converged (Moskos/Wood 1988). The consequence was a permanent, technologically advanced volunteer military, which became the largest employer in the US (Segal and Segal 2004: 5). With the abolishment of conscription, the military lost its privileged access to male recruits (Warner/Asch 2001).

The increased complexity of markets and technologies in the developing service economy professionalized the civilian sector as well. The foundation of the AVF was thus accompanied by increased competition between civilian and military employers over qualified personnel (Riche 2005: 23). Subsequent qualitative recruitment problems were partly solved by integrating women (ibid.: 16f.). These developments were paralleled by changes in gender-specific labor division in the civilian realm. Transformation from an industrial to a service economy furthered the workforce participation of women, loosening gender segregation on labor markets (Margolis 2000: 146ff.). As a result, more and more women became qualified for military occupations (Segal 1995: 768). Due to discrimination on the civilian labor market, women represented an ideal personnel reserve for the military, providing the increasingly needed, higher-qualified non-combatants (Riche 2005: 1). The military thus became an alternative to unemployment and social insecurity for women, too. These underlying social, technological, economic, and military processes were the basic conditions for integration into the military and have shaped its progression to the present day. They have also defined its boundaries.

Military personnel demands are the main determining factor in regard to forms and degrees of gender integration (Segal 1995: 757). Integration is thus a selective process which largely restricts women to areas in need of specialized personnel at lower and middle ranks. Gender policies, including different forms of combat exclusions, adapt participation to the varying needs of the institution. Remaining exclusions complicate the status of women in many areas by reducing demand and by discrimination in terms of pay, benefits, and promotions. Like on the civilian labor market, women dominate in jobs of medium quality that require a certain degree of qualification while offering minimal career prospects.

The 1990s represent a turning point in integration processes. Downsizing decreased personnel demands quantitatively, while requirements for education, training, and qualification were rising. The Persian Gulf War aggravated personnel shortages, particularly in support units for combat troops. The dependency on the female workforce promoted integration through comprehensive equality legislature, expanding roles in combat support. As a consequence, the mid-1990s saw an increase in representation during a phase of military downsizing and increased competition for promotion (Stiehm 1996: 56). This, in turn, furthered anti-integration sentiments. Women were again pushed back by official policy, assignment practices, and discriminatory behavior by commanders and comrades

(Harrell and Miller 1997). The military build-up for the "War on Terror" brought renewed efforts to recruit women. Significant new measures to further equality were, however, not introduced and even hindered in some areas. Integration can therefore not be conceptualized as linear progression; it includes fluctuations which also affect gender ideologies. Recruitment conditions play a role, as do political power relations and struggles between civilian and military leadership. These conflicts of interest shape the specific contents of general trends. They also determine whether integration is related to objectives of gender equality or designed solely to accommodate the military's demands.

Change of military gender ideologies

This study was designed to examine relations between structural developments and gender ideologies, which involved evaluating functions of these ideologies in stabilizing and changing the patterns of gender-specific division of labor. During the nineteenth and early twentieth century, dualistic gender stereotypes of "peaceful women" and "war-prone men" were established. The conditions for this were the separation of domestic and external (wage) labor, the nuclear family model in industrial capitalism, and the nationalization and militarization of warfare. Since the mid-twentieth century, technological progress and professionalization of warfare and production processes have transformed gender ideologies. Diversification of military work fields was followed by diversification of ideologies. The dichotomy of male warrior and female victim was supplemented by a multitude of gender images. As research on military masculinity has shown, various ideals coexist nowadays, depending on occupation and rank (Enloe 1988; Barrett 1999). Individualism, professionalism, and efficiency, which were considered increasingly relevant in civilian economy, were also revalued as military masculinity ideals. In the course of these developments, representations of military femininity diversified as well, supporting a complex system of gendered labor division. Images now range from the professional soldier to the patriotic heroine, from the sexualized intruder into the male bond to the victim in need of protection. Military, economic, and political conditions determine which images prevail.

The analysis of reporting on military gender issues in the NYT and the WP revealed one key consequence of the increased dependency on female personnel: the relative dominance of positive representations of military women and their integration within the examined media (Figure 5.1). The number of positive depictions in debates exceeded the negative ones during the investigated period by 63 percent to 37 percent, albeit strong fluctuations were observed between the different phases of this time frame. Military women were positively portrayed in 36 percent of statements and integration in 29 percent. Negative categories were less frequent: 19 percent of statements spoke negatively about military women and 18 percent about integration. As integration proceeded, negative depictions of female service members became less frequent compared to criticism of integration processes. Politicians and military representatives particularly refrained from negative statements on female personnel. Professionalization of military occupations and subsequent gender integration promoted their depiction as professional soldiers, but also as courageous and heroic warriors. More gender-neutral definitions of military professionalism and women in non-combat occupations became increasingly accepted, as Ruth Seifert (1996) has also shown for the German military. The convergence of male and female occupations on civilian and military labor markets decreased the importance of gender-specific attributions and increased the fluidity and "rationalization" of gender ideologies. The importance of traditional stereotypes in justifying inclusions and exclusions eroded, while individual achievement and efficiency became more relevant in argumentations. Professionalism was a central motive in debates throughout the investigated period. Arguments in favor of integration focused most often on its positive impact on military readiness and effectiveness, but values and normative orientations were also important points of reference in pro-argumentations.

Integration is a selective process largely determined by military personnel demands. Accordingly, traditional gender ideologies were still used to defend remaining boundaries. Jobs that were in high demand (e.g. leadership positions) or jobs with low qualification requirements (e.g. ground combat) were defended against competition from female personnel by utilizing traditional images of femininity and motherliness. The most negative attitudes were expressed towards the dual role of women as soldiers and (potential) mothers. In this context, it was combat rather than military service in general which became the ideological core of military masculinity. Leadership also remained a materially and discursively masculine domain (see also Seifert 1996). The reporting on military women therefore rarely featured them as responsible leaders or reliable comrades on the battlefield. Traditional male characteristics such as toughness and endurance were also hardly ascribed to them. Generally, camaraderie between men and women was seldom part of news stories, suggesting a strict gender-specific labor division in the services.

Resistance against integration by various social, political, and military groups was also expressed in negative attitudes and depictions. Opponents of integration focused even more on the effectiveness issue than supporters. They constructed a contradiction between integration and military demands, between ideals of equality and national security. Within these argumentations, they made use of traditional stereotypes. The role of women in the family mobilized the most resistance against integration, but lack of mental strength was also a common delegitimizing strategy. Military women were shown as weak, fearful, and mentally unprepared for the hardships of service. Prejudices referring to lack of physical abilities were comparatively rare, but consistently present in discourses. Public opinion was a central argument on both sides of the debate. In most instances, no data was given to support claims on the attitudes of the general public. Opponents frequently referred to the public's anti-integration sentiments as an argument for women's exclusion. In these populist appeals, the public was portrayed as sensitive, emotionally unable to handle women's service, and in need of protection from government and military representatives. The sensitivities of such a "feminized" public became a more important argument than the performance of women or pragmatic reasons for integration.

Overall, negative depictions of military women constituted a rather biologistic and culturalist discourse. The portrayals focused on the "naturally weaker sex" that required protection by men and, by extension, by the state and its laws. While positive depictions focused on the specific group of *military* women and their achievements, negative discourses more often referred to women in general and their "natural" qualities. It was deemed acceptable for military women to be courageous and aggressive, so that arguments for integration relied on achievements of those already in the services. The claim was not that all women were suitable for military service. In fact, arguments for integration sometimes claimed that most were not. Simultaneously, contra-arguments did not argue that military women were doing a bad job. They more often referred to the nature of womanhood in general and constructed it as oppositional to military culture. Whenever debates concentrated on integration processes rather than the women involved, discourses became more pragmatic: effectiveness, efficiency, and readiness were the key items. This was particularly valid for negative statement categories. Within positive ones, there was more room for value-oriented argumentation, expressed in more frequent referrals to equality, democracy, and modernization of cultural norms as the basis for integration. Journalists and politicians were most likely to use this kind of argumentation. Civil society representatives also tended to refer to cultural norms, but to different ones and for different purposes. The military most often spoke from an institutional perspective and relied on more pragmatic argumentation, in both positive and in negative evaluations.

Traditional gender images were also used to generally criticize military modernization, strategic reform, budget cuts, downsizing, and restructuring processes. Throughout the examined period, media reporting showed tendencies towards what Susan Jeffords (1989) has described as "remasculinization." Similar to the situation after the Vietnam War, military elites were confronted with a potential loss of power after the end of the Cold War. In this context, gender integration was interpreted as "civilization" and consequently as "feminization" of the US Armed Forces. As civilian and military occupations merged and the importance of traditional male characteristics in warfare decreased, media discourses often promoted nostalgia for a noble warrior masculinity of the past. Diplomatic conflict solutions and humanitarian interventions were also devalued as "effeminate." Similar attitudes were expressed in statements that denied women a "warrior ethos" or military sense of honor. It was claimed that they joined the military solely for pragmatic reasons such as career opportunities and educational benefits, whereas men allegedly only served out of patriotic motives. Integration was thus putting an end to the heroic masculine tradition of the US military.

These general effects of structural change were accompanied by considerable differences between the three phases of the investigated period (Figure 5.1). War affected the number and content of articles on military gender issues positively and produced many similarities between the early 1990s and the period after 2000. Accordingly, the positive coverage of integration functioned to mobilize for and justify war. Independently, integration inspired less media attention. War exerted a double influence in this regard: 1) it made recruitment environments tenser and thereby increased demand for female personnel, and 2) it provided the basis for utilizing images of military women in war propaganda. Under such circumstances, integration was frequently depicted as pragmatic and morally appropriate. Arguments about equality, democracy, progress, and military readiness were forwarded to defend integration measures. Images of courageous and emancipated female soldiers were contrasted to the Muslim women in the invaded countries. Historical efforts of women in the military were used to legitimize their present participation.[20] War also affected the contents of contra-arguments. During both interventions, the protection of women was a prevalent argument against integration, which complemented the protectionism towards Arab women that was claimed to be the reason for going to war.

The positive effects of war on media coverage of gender issues also reflected a shift in reporting patterns. During and around the event of war, the number of features on life on military bases and the "home front" rose. These mostly supported a positive image of military women and integration. If the proportion of features rose, so did positive trends. Reporting on "our troops" also made positive statements on military women the largest statement category. In both positive phases, supporters of integration tended to refer to character and achievement of female service members more often than to the anonymous process of integration. In turn, opponents also criticized the women rather than institutional processes. Trends towards personalization and individualization of war reporting, observed since the Vietnam War (Jeffords 1996), were reflected in these discursive patterns. War also increased the consensus between the two newspapers, aligning the contents of their reporting.

Despite many similarities between the early 1990s and the "War on Terror," reporting in these two phases differed considerably according to strategic context, political power relations, and gender policies in the civilian area. All these factors influenced how strongly military imperatives were promoted over the interests of women. Technological and professional warfare in a volunteer military generally produces more positive images of military women. In case of military defeat, scandals, or power losses of military institutions, however, problems are often interpreted as effects of gender integration, which is then constructed as a "demasculinization" of warfare, the Armed Forces, or the nation as a whole. These patterns were observed in reporting on the Somalia intervention and on the Abu Ghraib torture scandal. The late 1990s were generally shaped by these tendencies. Downsizing, job competition, and various "sex scandals" were expressed in discourses of lost masculinity and its possible rescue through women's exclusion.

The early 1990s

The early 1990s represent a phase of particularly frequent and particularly positive reporting. During this period, technological advances and the war in the Gulf led to a lack of qualified specialists (Segal 1995: 766; Warner/Asch 2001: 184). Additionally, limits set on women's participation impeded flexible troop assignment during the intervention. High media presence also made the public aware of increased female participation. As a consequence, many new positions and units were opened in the aftermath of the war, enforced by the Clinton administration. In this context, reporting peaked and was most positive in content. The professionalism of women and the efficiency of their integration were the most frequently used arguments and depictions.

One important discursive context for integration debates was general reporting on the war in the Gulf. New technology and professionalization promoted the image of the Armed Forces as a high-tech military led by efficient managers (Mariscal 1991: 106). In this context, group affiliations such as gender, and liberal values such as equality, were both less often represented in debates than individualistic arguments. New technologies were depicted as making war a gender-neutral phenomenon. This image of a modernized "corporate military" in which individual achievement and competence were key characteristics also included women as professional parts of the team. Performance thus became a key argument in pro-integration discourses. By drawing analogies to the civilian realm of business management, these features were claimed to automatically lead to equality. Equality as a value and goal in its own right became secondary. Overcoming out-dated values was supposed to modernize and normalize gender relations in the military. Other argumentative strategies of the early 1990s connected integration to the civil rights movement, presented public opinion as supportive of integration, showed military women who wanted to serve in combat, and criticized "protection" as a discriminatory argument. Women were depicted as combat-ready and their attitudes as relevant to military decision making. Because "liberation" of women in the Arab world became an important justification for interventions, they were also presented as a contrast to "oppressed" Muslim women. At the same time, images of the backward Muslim enemy promoted protectionist arguments against integration.

The issue of motherhood and military service was central in debates during this period. Changes in personnel demographics (higher average age, more service members with families, more marriages between service members) led to debates on the compatibility of family responsibilities and serving in a war. During the early 1990s, there was considerable resistance against portrayals of military women as "bad" mothers. These counter-arguments referred to values such as freedom of choice, reconciliation of job and family, and professional self-fulfillment. Feminist argumentation was also present in anti-integration discourses. The early 1990s were the only phase in which integration was criticized as anti-feminist. These arguments portrayed feminism as a pacifist movement which should support equality only in life-preserving jobs. Women were depicted primarily as victims of wars who should not be allowed to become perpetrators. Accordingly, feminists would be responsible to protect them from the military's grasp.

The late 1990s

When personnel demands dropped and competition for military jobs was high, negative representations increased. This was the case during the mid- to late-1990s, which deviated from generally positive trends. Implementation of integration measures and record female participation at a time when many (male) jobs were cut led to a negative reporting campaign. The "Republican Revolution" in Congress elections increased criticism of the Clinton administration's liberalization of military gender policy. Under these conditions, both pragmatic and normative arguments were put forward against integration. Note, however, that the negative trend in reporting reflected less an increase in negative statements than a decrease or absence of positive ones. One conclusion is that opposition to integration is a greater constant than support. The latter is mobilized only in phases of rising personnel demands.

During the later 1990s, the media's interest in military gender issues declined and reporting concentrated on various "sex scandals." Sexual morals and "biological constraints" were frequently used to argue against participation (see also Iskra 2007: 216ff.). While incidents of sexual harassment during the early 1990s, such as the "Tailhook scandal," had inspired sympathy and support for military women in the examined media, sexual violence was now discussed in a way which implicitly or explicitly blamed the victims and/or integration. Sexual abuse became a rationale for exclusion and was constructed as a necessary effect of military culture which could not be changed without harming military effectiveness. In these arguments, abuse became a logical result of integration and was thus trivialized as "natural."

Besides their role in "sex scandals," women were widely ignored in integration debates, which now focused mainly on institutional processes. The proportions between statements on military women and on integration began to shift. Negative statements on integration became the most frequent category, positive ones on military women the most infrequent. The later 1990s were thus characterized by a strong "institutional" perspective, reflecting a lack of reporting on interventions, military bases, and features on "our troops." At the same time, normative arguments gained momentum. Exclusion was less often represented as efficient, than as an American value offering protection from modernization processes. While the early 1990s had promoted integration as a way to overcome irrationalities and anachronisms in military culture and institutions, the late 1990s supported the maintenance of exclusion despite or even because of its irrationality. Women's performance and achievements were not denied, but constructed as insignificant in comparison to cultural considerations. Supporters also turned towards normative arguments and mentioned equality more often than effectiveness as a rationale for integration. The decreasing dependency on the female workforce and its flexible assignment diminished chances to argue for integration as a pragmatic measure. Without the opportunities to present integration as something that would benefit the military and the nation, the positive majority could not be sustained.

Downsizing, competition over jobs, and various cases of sexual misconduct strengthened discourses on lost military masculinity. In this context, women were construed as aberrations from the masculine ideals of military culture. Characteristic features of this phase were portrayals of military women as careerists. Here, women service members neither possessed the male qualities of heroism and dedication, nor did they conform to female stereotypes of self-sacrifice. War was thereby confirmed as a male sphere. The specifics of military life were highlighted, denying comparability to the civilian realm. The male bond was constructed as the core of military institutions, allowing for racial, but not for gender integration. Rising hostility towards military women was also mirrored in fewer statements featuring the protection argument. Exclusion was designed not to protect women from war, but to protect the military from women. Conflicts between civilian and military leadership were expressed in new constructions of integration. It became a measure of "political correctness" forced upon the military by "the feminists."

The "War on Terror"

The phase from 2000 to 2005 was shaped by specific political and strategic conditions which produced both similarities and differences with the early 1990s. Under the presidency of George W. Bush, military budgets and personnel size grew and the "War on Terror" supported militaristic imperatives in foreign and domestic policy. The interventions in Afghanistan and Iraq placed strategic emphasis on flexible ground combat. Ground combat, Special Forces, and private military companies (PMCs), from which women remain largely excluded, gained importance in the general strategic concept. Globalization of military labor markets and the marketization of warfare led to a remasculinization of warfare (Higate 2009: 4). At the same time, the war increased dependency on the female workforce, particularly in support units of ground combat forces. Integration was thus not reversed, despite the administration's generally anti-feminist gender policies. The opponents of integration did, however, achieve some major victories. DACOWITS, military women's most important representative, was devalued and new legislation strengthened Congressional control over military gender policy. Integration took place under different strategic and political conditions than during the early 1990s and was largely severed from gender equality imperatives.

Under these circumstances, the positive trend in reporting was less pronounced than during the early 1990s and the contents of positive depictions had changed. While the technological aerial warfare of 1991 had promoted images of professional, gender-neutral soldiers, the ground combat-based warfare during the "War on Terror" was expressed in representations of tough male warriors and women in need of protection. Because conservative values provided the basis for mobilization for the war, patriotism, faith, and heroism became more frequent points of reference in integration debates than professionalism and competence. Integration was justified as a patriotic measure, asserting the US' moral superiority.

Since emancipation and gender equality were also emphasized as a legitimization for war (Stabile/Kumar 2005, 765; Sjoberg/Gentry 2008; Masters 2009), exclusion of military women was presented as opposing the objectives of the war and endangering victory.

Effectiveness arguments were again overwhelmingly used in favor of integration. Their content, however, had shifted and the efficiency of an integrated military was reinterpreted: Traditionally "feminine" traits were supposed to serve military purposes, e.g. in dealing with the civilian population, and the enemy's anti-women sentiments were to be used as a strategic advantage. Reporting on the capture and rescue of US soldier Jessica Lynch serves as an example of how traditional gender ideologies were used to mobilize support for the war and at the same time maintain the military as a male resource of power. The cases of torture and abuse of Iraqi prisoners, with Abu Ghraib as the most prominent example, represent another form of instrumentalization of gender stereotypes that associate femininity with weakness and submission. Gender ideologies also played a role in the media representations of the torture. In the context of increased propagation of traditional family values, sexual violence against "the enemy" was interpreted as a reversal of "natural" gender roles, and the involved women were implicitly or explicitly held responsible for the scandal. Crises and problems during the intervention were again construed as "demasculinization." Anti-integration arguments also mirrored a strong emphasis on traditional gender roles and ideologies. Within these, military service of mothers had negative effects on families and society and, compared to the early 1990s, such claims were not countered. Portrayals of military women as masculinized and as careerists were used to construct them as a symbol for the demasculinization of the military, but also as a proof of their deviancy from traditional femininity ideals. The same function was fulfilled by images of them as particularly aggressive and cruel.

The "War on Terror" supported notions of an irrepressible male protective instinct which defined women as men's possessions and determined the boundaries of equality. In contrast to the early 1990s, these claims were not met with any meaningful counter-argumentation. Protectionism was accepted as an aspect of the war narrative. Images of a public supportive of integration almost disappeared from discourses. The perspective of military women themselves, be it positive or negative, was also no longer part of the debate. Neither were attitudes of male soldiers or husbands of military women. A collectivist and traditionally patriotic image of the military and of the intervention dominated the media during the "War on Terror." Compared to the early 1990s, representations were more frequently based upon dualistic gender ideologies and the notion of a strict gender-specific division of military tasks.

Groups of actors and lines of conflict

Military gender integration is a conflictuous process in which different groups inside and outside the military compete for influence and status. Their different interests are expressed in conflicts over the form and degree of integration in which different gender ideologies are used. Though the study focuses on a public meta-discourse, it also offers insights into the positions of different groups of social, political, and military actors. Journalists contributed the greatest proportion of statements to media debates (65 percent). Among these, positive statements were overrepresented at 69 percent. Distinguishing characteristics of their argumentations were the emphasis on performance, gender equality, and modernization of values. Military effectiveness played a less significant role than normative arguments, and in the positive and negative categories the focus lay on women rather than on integration processes. War had a strong positive influence on the quantity and quality of their participation in debates. In peacetime, journalists' contributions decreased, partially reflecting shifts in genre representation, and their statements became by majority negative. Trends in the contents of their statements paralleled politicians' contributions rather than that of military and civil society representatives. In contrast to politicians and military leaders, they tended to personalize debates, concentrating on depictions of individual women rather than on structural contexts.

Civilian politicians were most interested in military women in times of foreign policy crises. Generally, they contributed only 8 percent to the debates, but the positive majority of their statements was overwhelming (80 percent). They focused more on the integration process than on military women and were the only group to not make negative statements about female service members. Criticism of the female troops was considered a political taboo. The contributions of politicians depended mostly on whether the Armed Forces were serving in a war or not. During war, politicians mobilized women by arguing in favor of their competence, necessary social change, and equality as an objective of war. Their participation was overwhelmingly positive then: 90 percent positive statements during the early 1990s and 85 percent during the "War on Terror." In these phases, Republicans and Democrats both supported integration by majority, though Democratic Congressmen and -women contributed most to positive trends. In peace time, political proponents of integration from both parties remained almost totally silent (or were no longer cited in the media). Though war was the key factor in politicians' representation in media discourses, political power relations and gender policy in the civilian realm were also influential. During the early 1990s, when government and Congress were both dominated by the Democratic Party, statements from the Pentagon, DACOWITS, and civilian leaders in military personnel management strengthened positive trends among politicians' contributions. After the Republican Party had taken over Congress, only Republican voices against integration were raised in media debates; this viewpoint constituted 100 percent of politicians' statements in the second half of the 1990s. This changed again with the "War on Terror," when supporters of integration from both parties took the lead in debates again. Under the condition of Republican rule, positive trends were, however, less pronounced. Politicians' statements thus fluctuated drastically. Support was only mobilized in politically opportune times, when it served the war effort and/or when equality was promoted by the leading party in the civilian realm.

The military contributed 10 percent to overall reporting, but throughout the investigated time period their contributions declined from 13 percent to 7 percent. Though the investigated material cannot grasp the military's overall position on integration, the reconstruction of its participation in media debates allows for some interpretation. One central line of conflict ran between military and civilian leadership. The main issue here was not primarily whether more or less integration would be appropriate, but who controls military personnel policy. The military's statements mainly attempted to defend flexibility and independence in personnel issues against civilian politics, "public opinion," and democratic institutions. Unsurprisingly, the institutional perspective prevailed and military representatives spoke more often about integration than about military women. Both positive and negative arguments focused on military necessity, readiness, and efficiency. Positive statements on integration were the largest group. Negative statements featured the protection of women as a US value, women's mental weakness, and the incompatibility of motherhood and military service.

Overall, the military's statements were only 56 percent positive, but became more positive during the course of the analyzed period: from 41 percent positive in the early 1990s to 75 percent in the late 1990s to 80 percent after 2000. These patterns did not conform to general trends and even contradicted them in some aspects: The military was by majority negative during the overwhelmingly positive phase of the early 1990s, as it fought politically motivated equality measures. During the negative phase of late 1990s, it was the only group to evaluate integration positively by majority. Long-term dependency on female personnel and negative publicity due to sexual violence within the services led to a defense of integration even in times of generally negative reporting and increased criticism. During the "War on Terror," the military again fought political interventions. This time, however, politicians were not engaging for more equality, but for women's exclusion from specific units. These conservative initiatives to install new restrictions were not compatible with personnel requirements and thus publicly rejected by the affected parts of the military. The result was more positive statements on military women, featuring their courage and competence and demanding that they not be demoralized.

Integration therefore cannot be conceptualized as a politically motivated intrusion from outside. Notions of a backward military that has to be forced to integrate women do not correspond to the complex reality of integration processes. The political context is equally important for interpreting the military's statements as solely strategic considerations and personnel requirements. Though these latter factors are influential, they do not translate one-to-one into media representations. Moreover, the military is not a unified actor. The impacts of modernization and the dependency on the female workforce differ according to service, occupation, and rank. Debates on gender integration thus mark horizontal and vertical conflict lines within the military. Restructuring led to a loss of power for traditional military elites and occupations; it also increased competition between the services over the defense budget. Men in technologically less advanced working areas and on lower ranks, who experienced direct competition from better-qualified female personnel and whose occupational areas were devalued in strategic concepts, were most likely to interpret organizational modernization as "demasculinization."

High female participation rates were not sufficient reason for a service to propagate positive images of military women in the media. The most positive statements came from the Army. Its ratio of women was lower than that of the Air Force and, at times, the Navy, and it has a relatively high proportion of ground combat forces. Still, it relies on female labor in support units and suffers most from recruitment shortages. This made the Army the most active in pro-integration discourses. The Navy's statements were also positive, but less overwhelmingly. Despite their large support structure, their demand for a female workforce is smaller because they are less affected by recruitment problems. The Air Force, which has the highest female participation rate and is the most technologically advanced service, contributed most negatively to debates: it was even less affected by recruitment problems, and competition for its top positions was strong. The Marines were also by majority negative, but to a lesser degree. Low women's representation, strong competition over jobs, small support structure, and high proportion of ground combat troops led to the negative prevalence, but also to minimal participation in debates.

During the study period, interests against women's participation were increasingly organized outside of the military which was reflected in media discourses. Representatives of civil society contributed 16 percent of statements to debates, i.e. more than military and political actors. They were also the only group whose statements were by majority negative (69 percent). Most often, they spoke negatively about integration, most seldom positively about military women. Their participation in the two positive phases (1990–1994, 2000–2005) was much lower (14 percent and 10 percent) than during the negative phase (30 percent; 1995–1999). In the late 1990s, when chances for implementing anti-women measures were higher, anti-integration organizations and individuals were most active. Supporters withdrew from debates or had no access to media discourses.

Until the late 1990s, statements from independent representatives of civil society (scholars, intellectuals, writers, etc.) prevailed over representatives of organizations. In that time period, feminist activists who argued against integration out of a anti-militarist perspective gained marginal access to media debates. This changed after 2000, when two thirds of statements already came from NGOs, think tanks, and consultant firms. This no doubt included "outsourcing" of anti-feminist claims from groups within the military and politics to the seemingly private sector. Neoconservative think tanks and lobbyists such as the Center for Military Readiness (CMR) and the Eagle Forum, whose influence in Washington increased during the Bush Junior administration, openly fought integration by invoking the role of women as mothers, issues of sexual morals, lack of psychological suitability, and the protection of women as an important American value. They presented themselves as advocates of the military against civilian politics, but also as representatives of "public opinion" and "common sense." In the case of the CMR, sponsoring from parts of the Army has become public (Priest 1997b). Support for women in the services was also organized within NGOs and political consultant companies such as the National Organization for Women (NOW) or the Women's Research and Education Institute (WREI). Their representatives, however, were cited far less in the media than their counterparts.

Which ideologies were successfully promoted by what groups depended on the respective social, political, and military frameworks. During the early 1990s, civilian politicians, women's groups inside and outside the military, and technologically advanced sectors of the military managed to enforce professionalism, individualism, and competence as hegemonic images of military women. The high-tech war in the Persian Gulf and an administration that enforced gender equality in the services enabled new legislation and rising female representation. The late 1990s marked a renewed shift characterized by military downsizing, absence of major interventions, and a Republican majority in Congress. These conditions enabled opposing voices to take the lead in debates on integration. Politicians who had earlier advocated equality measures withdrew from the debate, and lobbyists fighting integration came to dominate the scene. The conditions in the early twenty-first century once again supported groups in favor of women's military participation. The interventions of the "War on Terror" generally increased personnel demands and necessitated flexible assignment and deployment. Neoconservative power gains, anti-feminist politics in the civilian realm, growing military budgets, and an intervention legitimized by referring to a "clash of cultures" supported the instrumentalization of traditional femininity ideologies in warfare. Military imperatives were prioritized over civil rights. Under these conditions, integration was not reversed but put under Congressional control and institutionally and discursively disconnected from equality agendas.

Military gender ideologies are a product of social, military, and political processes. As such, they attain different functions for domestic and foreign policy discourses. Positive and negative images of military women are instrumentalized to argue for group interests in integration debates, but also in general debates on gender relations and policies, in debates on military reform, strategic concepts, and current interventions. They can either be used to criticize or to support military and political leadership, rationales for interventions, and certain security or gender policies. While gender ideologies in integration debates are functional for these other discourses, gender ideologies in war reporting or other debates are also to be read as contribution to integration discourses. Military women predominantly become an issue in the media when it serves the positive portrayal of the nation, the military, and the current war effort. They are portrayed particularly favorably when their images can be utilized for war propaganda. An important function of these images is the representation of an opposition to Muslim culture and the legitimization of war to free "oppressed" women in the Arab world. These discourses, however, also underscore masculinist protectionism at home and strengthen anti-integration arguments that refer to women's necessary protection. Especially during the "War on Terror," they invoked images of the state as a protective patriarch who has to curtail citizenship rights for the public good, wage war on a country to free its women (Young 2003), and exclude its "own" women from military participation due to security reasons.

Gender, state, and the military

The analysis of military gender ideologies highlights the effects of state transformations on gender relations and the role of the state and the military as producers of gender ideology. Historically, a strong connection is evident between state formation, militarization of warfare, and dualistic gender ideologies. This connection inscribed gender dichotomies into state institutions and provided the basis for women's exclusion from political and military participation. Under conditions of centralized state-control over recruitment and economic dependence on industrial production, nationalization and centralization of warfare curtailed women's participation. Under conditions of technological advancement and professionalization in military and civilian sectors, the military opens up towards women. This trend has recently been countervailed by tendencies towards denationalization and privatization of warfare. As military professionalism and diversification increase in a globalized economy, the state partially withdraws from recruitment and military labor markets are transformed.

One effect of military privatization is that decision-making on personnel issues becomes less democratic: the decisive power over the deployment of PMCs lies with the executive branch and not with Congress (Avant and Sigelman 2009). While Congress seeks to expand its influence on female participation in the regular forces, sometimes with success, it has little or no control over privately employed troops. Note, however, that democratic control over military gender issues does not necessarily equate with better conditions for women, as the past has frequently shown. While Congress further supports limitations on their participation and their inferior status in the regular services, a primarily masculine world of privatized security has developed. Although data on the effects of privatization on women's military labor market participation are scarce, there is little evidence that neo-liberalization of labor markets benefits their status as state or private military personnel. While women gained admission to the regular forces and were able to attain a certain degree of equality therein, a new male-dominated military labor market has developed, which is largely uncontrolled by the state. The upgrading of PMCs within military strategy represents a remasculinization of warfare in an allegedly state-free zone.

These results show that the relationship between the material and the cultural, between labor division, political power relations, and ideology is still a worthwhile object of study for gender research and theory. A materialist approach to gender phenomena—one that emphasizes social and political structures and patterns of labor division—can be successfully applied to issues of war and the military. Such a perspective yields consistent explanations for changes in military gender ideologies and sharpens the focus on continuities and discontinuities in these ideologies. It helps bridge the gap between research on the structural and institutional change on the one side, and research on changes in military culture and gender ideology on the other. Finally, it draws attention to conflicts between different groups of social actors who utilize military gender ideologies to further their interests. This is a key step forward in identifying the structural context variables that influence the functionality and relative success of these ideologies. The results also provide the basis for research on gender ideologies in other (state) institutions.

Notes

1 All translations of German citation by author.
2 The beginning of Cultural Studies (with capital letters) can be traced to the work of Raymond Williams, Richard Hoggart, E.P. Thompson, and Stuart Hall and has its institutional center in Birmingham, at the "Center for Contemporary Cultural Studies" (CCCS).
3 Williams' concept is an approach to media theory and is not related to Harris' research strategy of Cultural Materialism (Harris 1979).
4 The *NYT*'s circulation from 1998 to 2005 lay between 1,066,658 and 1,194,491 copies. It is therefore the third largest nationwide daily newspaper following *USA Today and The Wall Street Journal* (Audit Bureau of Circulations 2009).
5 The *WP* is the largest daily and highest circulation newspaper in the Washington, D.C., area. Despite its high profile, it is defined as a local newspaper, specializing in reporting on the US government, White House, and Congress. Between 1995 and 2005, its circulation was about 750,000 copies on weekdays (The Awl 2009).
6 Articles on the status of military women, on planned or implemented policy changes, on debates in Congress, commissions, committees, and within the military, and on statements from military and political elites as well as representatives of civil society.
7 Reporting from military bases and soldiers' hometowns; portrayals of military leaders, "heroes," and "ordinary soldiers".
8 Opinionated articles by editors, journalists, and guest commentators.
9 Categorization within a genre is not always definite. Reports can contain elements of a feature to illustrate a certain point or can strongly argue for an opinion. At the same time, features and editorials can cite statements from politicians or depict developments of debates and policies. The classification therefore followed the newspaper's own categorization or, if none was given, the predominant characteristics of the article.
10 This means that more articles contained the search keys than were actually analyzed. However, the total number of search results rose and fell in a similar pattern as the number of analyzed articles. Years that featured daily reporting on court proceedings in high profile cases of sexual harassment within the military were an exception.
11 Karin Hausen (1976) has also shown the general patterns of these processes in a case study of Germany, where similar developments had already begun around the mid-nineteenth century. Here, too, the concept of family had originally included economic production and domestic workers. With the emergence of the bourgeois nuclear family, housework lost its connection to productive work. It was no longer defined as work, but as a natural condition. Female and male tasks were continuously diverging, which was reinforced by separate educational paths. These structural changes were supported by the ideology of "Geschlechtscharaktere" (gender characters) which constructed "natural" characteristics of men and women as compatible with their different fields of activity.

12   Hegemonic family ideals concealed that many women participated actively in the process of industrial production as workers. The bourgeois housewife became the standard of femininity.

13   For a detailed analysis of the symbolic relevance of rape as a war crime, see Seifert 2006.

14   Most recruits were not drafted, even before 1973. Only the Army recruited conscripted personnel, whereas other services consisted entirely of volunteers.

15   The fluctuation of enlisted personnel decreased from 21.1 percent per year in 1973 to 15 percent in the late 1980s. The average duration of military service for enlisted troops increased from 4.7 years in 1973 to 6.5 years in 1988. The proportion of personnel with more than four years of work experience rose from 39 percent to 50 percent (Warner/Asch 2001: 179).

16   While personnel costs made up 34.2 percent of military expenses at the height of the Vietnam War, they were only 27.3 percent in 1998.

17   Around half of all service members are under the age of 25 (Segal/Segal 2004: 23).

18   1,000 US military women participated in the UN intervention in Somalia between 1992 and 1994. A total of 1,200 took part in the 1995 intervention in Haiti (WREI n.d.).

19   16,300 single parents, most of them men, and 1,200 military couples participated in Operation Desert Storm (Priest 1991).

20   According to Segal (1995: 761), this is a global phenomenon: "[W]hen the armed forces need women, their prior military history is recalled to demonstrate that they can perform effectively in various positions. ... In the aftermath of war women's military activities are reconstructed as minor (or even nonexistent)." It might not be a coincidence that the memorial for female Vietnam veterans that had been demanded for some time was finally realized during the early 1990s.

References

Adorno, T. W. (1974) *Philosophische Terminologie: Zur Einleitung*, Vol. 2, Frankfurt am Main: Suhrkamp.

Adorno, T. W. and Horkheimer, M. (1947) *Dialektik der Aufklärung: Philosophische Fragmente*, Amsterdam: Querido.

Albrecht-Heide, A. (1988) "Women and War: Victims and Collaborators," in E. Isaksson (ed.) *Women and the Military System*, New York: St Martin's Press.

Allen, H. (1992) "The Matter-of-Fact Major's War Story," *The Washington Post*, August 8, f.01.

Althusser, L. (1977) *Ideologie und ideologische Staatsapparate*, Hamburg: VSA.

Altvater, E. (2006) "Die zerstörerische Schöpfung. Kapitalistische Entwicklung zwischen Zivilisierung und Entzivilisierung," *PROKLA. Zeitschrift für kritische Sozialwissenschaft*, Vol. 143, No. 2, 157–75.

Angrist, J. (1995) "Using Social Security Data on Military Applicants to Estimate the Effect of Voluntary Military Service on Earnings," *Nationals Bureau of Economic Research Working Paper Series*, 5192, x–50.

Applebaum, A. (2003) "When Women Go to War," *The Washington Post*, March 26, A.17.

Armor, D. (1996) "Race and Gender in the US Military," *Armed Forces & Society*, Vol. 23, No. 1, 7–27.

Armor, D. and Gilroy, C. (2007) "Changing Minority Representation in the U.S. Military," unpublished manuscript, published in *Armed Forces & Society* (2010), Vol. 36, No. 2, 223–46.

Asch, B., Orvis, B., Sastry, N., Kilburn, R., Klerman, J. A., Murray, M. and McDonald, L. (2001) *Military Recruiting. Trends, Outlooks, and Implications*, RAND Corporation Report.

Associated Press (1993) "2 Killed in Somalia Are to Get Medal of Honor," *The New York Times*, May 15, 1/29.

Associated Press (2003a) "Details Released of Lynch Rescue," 5 April. Available at <http://www.foxnews.com/story/0,2933,83288,00.html> (accessed February 26, 2004).

Associated Press (2003b) "Former POW Jessica Lynch Set for Return Home," July 22. Available at <http://www.foxnews.com/story/0,2933,92567,00.html> (accessed February 26, 2004).

Associated Press (2004) "Former Abu Ghraib Unit Returns Home," *The New York Times*, August 3, A8.

Audit Bureau of Circulations (2009) *The New York Times Circulation Data*. Available at <http://www.nytco.com/investors/financials/nyt-circulation.html> (accessed December 16, 2009)

Avant, D. and Sigelman, L. (2009) "What Does Private Security in Iraq Mean for US Democracy?," conference paper, *Annual Convention of the International Studies Association*, February 15–18, New York.

The Awl (2009) *A Graphic History of Newspaper Circulation Over the Last Two Decades*, October 26. Available at <http://www.theawl.com/2009/10/a-graphic-history-of-newspaper-circulation-over-the-last-two-decades> (accessed December 21, 2009).

Baker, R. (1997) "First It's About Killing," *The New York Times*, June 7, 119.

Barrett, F. J. (1999) "Die Konstruktion hegemonialer Männlichkeit in Organisationen: Das Beispiel der US-Marine," in C. Eifler and R. Seifert (eds) *Soziale Konstruktionen. Militär und Geschlechterverhältnisse*, Münster: Westfälisches Dampfboot, 71–91.

Barrett, M. (1997) "Ideology and the Cultural Production of Gender," in R. Hennessy and C. Ingraham (eds) *Materialist Feminism. A Reader in Class, Difference, and Women's Lives*, London: Routledge, 88–94.

Becker, E. (1999) "Motherhood Deters Women From Army's Highest Ranks," *The New York Times*, November 29, A1.

Becker-Schmidt, R. (2008). "'Class,' 'gender,' 'ethnicity,' 'race': Logiken der Differenzsetzung, Verschränkungen von Ungleichheitslagen und gesellschaftliche Strukturierung," in C. Klinger *et al.* (eds) *Achsen der Ungleichheit. Zum Verhältnis von Klasse, Geschlecht und Ethnizität*, Frankfurt am Main: Campus, 56–83.

Belknap, M. H. (2001) *The CNN Effect: Strategic Enabler or Operational Risk?* Pennsylvania: USAWC Strategy Research Project, US Army War College.

Bellafair, J. L. (2006) "Public Role Models: The First Women of the Defense Advisory Committee on Women in the Services," *Armed Forces & Society*, Vol. 32, No. 3, 424–36.

Benson, R. and Hallin, D. C. (2007) "How States, Markets and Globalization Shape the News. The French and US National Press, 1965–1997," *European Journal of Communication*, Vol. 22, No. 1, 27–48.

Binkin, M. (1986) *Military Technology and Defense Manpower*, Washington: The Brookings Institute.

Blanchard, J. (2004) "War Romance Passionate in "Wedding," *The Washington Times*, August 13, D03.

Booth, B., Falk, W. W., Segal, M. W. and Segal, D. (2000) "The Impact of Military Presence in Local Labor Markets on the Employment of Women," *Gender and Society*, Vol. 14, No. 2, 318–32.

Bourdieu, P. (1986) "The forms of capital," in J. Richardson (ed.) *Handbook of Theory and Research for the Sociology of Education*, New York: Greenwood, 241–58.

Brah, A. and Phoenix, A. (2004) "Ain't I A Woman? Revisiting Intersectionality," *Journal of International Women's Studies*, Vol. 5, No. 3, 75–86.

Britt, D. (2004) "Athena in Iraq: Women at War Air Evil Truth," *The Washington Post*, May 7, B.01.

Brooke, J. (1997) "New Attention to Women in Military," *The New York Times*, March 3, A10.

Brown, M. (2006) "'A Woman in the Army Is Still a Woman.' Recruiting Women into the All-Volunteer Force," conference paper, *Annual Convention of the International Studies Association*, March 22–25, San Diego.

Burke, C. (1996) "Pernicious Cohesion," in J. Stiehm (ed.) *It's Our Military, Too. Women and the US Military*, Philadelphia: Temple University Press, 205–19.

Caldwell, R. A. and Mestrovic, S. (2008) "The Role of Gender in "Expressive" Abuse at Abu Ghraib," *Cultural Sociology*, Vol. 2, No. 3, 275–99.

Carneiro, R. L. (1994) "War and Peace. Alternating Realities in Human History," in S. P. Reyna, and R. E. Downs (eds) *Studying War. Anthropological Perspectives*, Langhorne: Gordon and Breach, 3–27.

Carreiras, H. (2006) *Gender and the Military: Women and the Armed Forces in Western Democracies* (Cass Military Studies), London and New York: Routledge.

Cave, D. (2005) "Normally Quiet, a Military Town Talks of Casualties," *The New York Times*, June 27, A1.

Chavez, L. (1993) "The First Generation of Draft Daughters?," *The Washington Post*, July 11, C3.

Chesterman, S. (2007) *From Mercenaries to Market: The Rise and Regulation of Private Military Companies*, New York: Oxford University Press.

Chinni, D. (2003) *Jessica Lynch: Media Myth Making in the Iraq War*. Available at <http://www.journalism.org/resources/research/reports/war/postwar/lynch.asp> (accessed Febuary 26, 2004).

Cockburn, C. (1998) *The Space Between Us: Negotiating Gender and National Identities in Conflict*, London and New York: Zed Books.

Cohn, C. (2000) "How Can She Claim Equal Rights When She Doesn't Have to Do as Many Push-Ups as I Do?": The Framing of Men's Opposition to Women's Equality in the Military," *Men and Masculinities*, Vol. 3, No. 2, 131–51.

Coker, C. (2001) *Humane Warfare: The New Ethics of Postmodern War*, London and New York: Routledge.

— (2002) *Waging War Without Warriors: The Changing Culture of Military Conflict*, Boulder: Lynne Rienner Publishers.

Colford, P. D. and Siemasko C. (2003) "Fiends Raped Jessica," *The New York Daily News*, 6 February. Available at <http://www.nydailynews.com/front/story/134264p-119598c.html> (accessed February 26, 2004).

Crenshaw, K. (1991) "Mapping the Margins. Intersectionality, Identity Politics, and Violence against Women of Color," *Stanford Law Review*, Vol. 43, No. 6, 1241–99.

Cushman, J. (1993a) "Top Admiral Backs Full Combat Roles Form Women in Navy," *The New York Times*, April 5, A1.

Cushman, J. (1993b) "The Navy's Latest on Jobs for Women," *The New York Times*, April 11, 43.

Davenport, C. and Amon, M. (2004) "Accused Soldiers a Diverse Group," *The Washington Post*, May 9, A18.

DeGroot, G. J. and Peniston-Bird, C. M. (2001) *A Soldier and a Woman: Women in the Military*, Harlow: Longman.

Devine, D. (2004) "Torture Scandal Fingerprints," *The Washington Times*, May 11. Available at <http://www.washtimes.com/commentary/20040511-085209-9538r.htm> (accessed July 30, 2004).

Dörner, A. (1997) "Medienkultur und politische Öffentlichkeit: Perspektiven und Probleme der Cultural Studies aus politikwissenschaftlicher Sicht," in A. Hepp and R. Winter (eds) *Kultur. Medien. Macht. Cultural Studies und Medienanalyse*, Opladen: Westdeutscher Verlag, 319–35.

Duffield, M. (2005) *Global Governance and the New Wars: The Merging of Development and Security*, London and New York: Zed Books.

Duke, L. (2004) "A Woman Apart," *The Washington Post*, September 19, D01.

Dunsmore, B. (1996) *The Next War: Live?* Discussion Paper D-22, John F. Kennedy School of Government.

Editorial (1991) "America's Fighting Women," *The New York Times*, August 5, A12.

— (1992a) "Women and Stone Age Warriors," *The New York Times*, July 8, A18.

— (1992b) "Women in Combat: Maybe? Yes?," *The New York Times*, November 28, 118.

— (1993a) "Aspin Is to Set Women's Role In All Services," *The New York Times*, April 8, D20.

— (1993b) "Women and War," *The New York Times*, April 12, A16.

— (2003) "The Pinking of Armed Forces," *The New York Times*, March 24.

— (2005) "Chauvinism at the Battlefront," *The New York Times*, May 20, A24.

Editorial (1990) "A Combat Soldier Named Linda," *The Washington Post*, January 6, a.20.

— (1992) "Women in Combat? No," *The Washington Post*, November 28, a.21.

— (1993) "Moving Military Women Ahead," *The Washington Post*, April 8, a.20.

— (1994) "Women Soldiers, Step by Step," *The Washington Post*, January 9, c.06.

— (1997) "Women in the Military," *The Washington Post*, May 1, A.22.

— (2005a) "Women at War," *The Washington Post*, May 18, A.16.

— (2005b) "Women in the Military," *The Washington Post*, May 24, A16.

Egan, T. (1996) "A Battleground of Sexual Conflict," *The New York Times*, November 15, A14.

Eifler, C. and Seifert, R. (eds) (1999) *Soziale Konstruktionen. Militär und Geschlechterverhältnis*, Münster: Westfälisches Dampfboot.

Elshtain, J. B. (1987) *Women and War*, Chicago: University of Chicago Press.

Elwell, F. (1991) *The Evolution of the Future*, New York: Greenwood.

Embser-Herbert, M. S. (2004) "When Women Abuse Power, Too," *The Washington Post*, May 16, B.01.

Enloe, C. (1988) "Beyond 'Rambo': Women and the Varieties of Militarized Masculinity," in E. Isaksson (ed.) *Women and the Military System*, New York: St Martin's Press, 71–93.

— (1990) *Bananas, Beaches, and Bases: Making Feminist Sense of International Politics*, Berkeley/Los Angeles/London: University of California Press.

— (2000) *Maneuvers: The International Politics of Militarizing Women's Lives*, Berkeley/Los Angeles/London: University of California Press.

Fainaru, S. (2005) "Silver Stars Affirm One Unit's Mettle," *The Washington Post*, May 26, A.01.

Fears, D. (2004) "Military Families Mourn Daughters," *The Washington Post*, May 26, A.01.

Feaver, P. and Kohn, R. (2001) *Soldiers and Civilians: The Civil-Military Gap and American National Security*, Boston: MIT Press.

Ferguson, R. B. (ed.) (1984) *Warfare, Culture, and Environment*, Orlando: Academic Press.

Finlay, B. (2006) *George W. Bush and the War on Women*, London and New York: Zed Books.

Fisher, M. (2004) "Vile Photos Miss The Rot Behind A Few Bad Apples," *The Washington Post*, May 13, B01.

Foucault, M. (1980) *Power/Knowledge: Selected Interviews and Other Writings 1972–1977*, New York: Pantheon Books.

Franklin, B. H. (1994). "From Realism to Virtual Reality. Images of America's Wars," in S. Jeffords and L. Rabinovitz (eds) *Seeing Through the Media. The Persian Gulf War*, New Brunswick: Rutgers University Press, 25–43.

Fraser, N. (2004) "Feministische Politik im Zeitalter der Anerkennung: Ein zweidimensionaler Ansatz für Geschlechtergerechtigkeit," in J. Beerhorst, A. Demirovic, and M. Guggemos (eds) *Kritische Theorie im gesellschaftlichen Strukturwandel*, Frankfurt am Main: Suhrkamp, 453–76.

Frevert, U. (1996) "Soldaten, Staatsbürger. Überlegungen zur historischen Konstruktion von Männlichkeit," in T. Kühne (ed.) *Männergeschichte—Geschlechtergeschichte. Männlichkeit im Wandel der Moderne*, Frankfurt am Main: Campus, 69–87.

Gabbert, K. (2007) *Gleichstellung—zu Befehl! Der Wandel der Geschlechterverhältnisse im US-Militär*, Frankfurt am Main: Campus.

Garnham, N. (1983) "Toward a Theory of Cultural Materialism," *Journal of Communication*, Vol. 33, No. 3, 314–29.

Gellman, B. (1992) "Panel Seeks to Limit Women in Combat," *The Washington Post*, November 4, a.03.

Gerhart, A. (2002) "The Air Force Flier in the Ointment," *The Washington Post*, January 7, C.01.

Ghani, A. and Lockhart, C. (2009), *Fixing Failed States: A Framework for Rebuilding a Fractured World*, New York: Oxford University Press.

Gibbons, M. S. (2004) "White Trash: A Class Relevant Scapegoat for the Cultural Elite," *Journal of Mundane Behavior*, Vol. 5, No. 1. Available at <mundanebehavior.org/issues/V5n1/gibbons.htm> (accessed April 27, 2005).

Gilbert, P. (2003) *New Terror, New Wars*, Edinburgh: Edinburgh University Press.

Goff, Stan (2003) "The Use and Abuse of a Woman Soldier. Jessica Lynch, Plural," *Counterpunch*, December 13/14. Available at <http://www.counterpunch.org/goff1 2132003.html> (accessed February 26, 2004).

Goldstein, J. (2001) *War and Gender: How Gender Shapes the War System and Vice Versa*, Cambridge: Cambridge University Press.

Gonzales, D. (1991) "So Few Died, but How It Hurt Those Back Home: 11 Stories," *The New York Times*, March 15, B4.

Goodman, E. (2001) "From Burqas to Abayas," *The Washington Post*, December 8, A.25.

— (2004) "Unfriendly Fires in the Gender Wars," *The Washington Post*, April 10, A.15.

Gordon, M. (1992) "Military Chiefs Admit Need to Curb Sexual Harassment," *The New York Times*, July 31, A10.

Gordon, M. R. and Cushman, J. H. (1993) "Mission in Somalia: After Supporting Hunt for Aidid, US Is Blaming UN for Losses," *The New York Times,* October 18, A1.

Gramsci, A. (1999) *Gefängnishefte: Kritische Gesamtausgabe*, Vol. 7, Hamburg: Argument-Verlag.

Gray, J. (1959) *The Warriors: Reflections on Men in Battle*, New York: Hartcourt Brace.

Gutman, S. (1997) "The Great Umbrella Debate," *The New York Times*, October 9, A31.

Hacker, B. C. (1981) "Women and Military Institutions in Early Modern Europe. A Reconnaissance," *Signs: Journal of Women in Culture and Society*, Vol. 6, No. 4, 643–71.

Hackworth, D. (1991) "Women Warriors," *The Washington Post*, October 4, a.25.

Hagemann, K. (1999) "Venus und Mars. Reflexionen zu einer Geschlechtergeschichte von Militär und Krieg," in C. Eifler and Frauenbündnisprojekt Osnabrück (eds) *Militär-Gewalt-Geschlechterverhältnis*, Osnabrück, 8–40.

Hagemann, K. and Pröve, R. (eds) (1998) *Landsknechte, Soldatenfrauen und Nationalkrieger. Militär, Krieg und Geschlechterordnung im historischen Wandel*, Frankfurt am Main: Suhrkamp.

Hall, S. (1983) "The Problem of Ideology. Marxism Without Guarantees," in B. Matthews (ed.) *Marx: A Hundred Years on*, London: Lawrence & Wishart, 57–85.

Hallin, D. C. (1984) "The Media, the War in Vietnam, and Political Support: A Critique of the Thesis of an Oppositional Media," *The Journal of Politics*, Vol. 46, No. 1, 2–24.

Hämmerle, C. (2000) "Von den Geschlechtern der Kriege und des Militärs. Forschungseinblicke und Bemerkungen zu einer neuen Debatte," in T. Kühne and B. Ziemann (eds) *Was ist Militärgeschichte?*, Paderborn: Schöningh, 229–62.

Hanson, C. (2002) "Women Warriors. How the Press Has Helped and Hurt the Battle for Equality," *Columbia Journalism Review*, May/June, 1–5.

Harders, C. (2004) "Neue Kriegerinnen. Lynndie England und Jessica Lynch," *Blätter für deutsche und internationale Politik*, 09, 1101–11.

Harrell, M. and Miller, L. (1997) *New Opportunities for Military Women. Effects Upon Readiness, Cohesion, and Morale*, RAND Corporation Report.

Harris, M. (1979) *Cultural Materialism. The Struggle for a Science of Culture*, New York: Vintage Books.

— (1984) "A Cultural Materialist Theory of Band and Village Warfare. The Yanomamo Test," in R. B. Ferguson (ed.) *Warfare, Culture, and Environment*, Orlando: Academic Press, 111–40.

— (1994) "Cultural Materialism is Alive and Well and Won't Go Away Until Something Better Comes Along," in R. Borofsky (ed.) *Assessing Cultural Anthropology*, New York: McGraw-Hill.

— (2001/1968) *The Rise of Anthropological Theory. A History of Theories of Culture*, Walnut Creek, CA: Alta Mira Press.

Hart Sinnreich, R. (2001) "Fit for Duty. With No Gender Compromises," *The Washington Post*, August 19, B.07.

Hausen, K. (1976) "Die Polarisierung der 'Geschlechtscharaktere': Eine Spiegelung der Dissoziation von Erwerbs- und Familienleben," in W. Conze (ed.) *Sozialgeschichte der Familie in der Neuzeit*, Stuttgart: Klett, 363–93.

Heinrich, M. (1991; 2nd edn 1999) *Die Wissenschaft vom Wert. Die Marxsche Kritik der politischen Ökonomie zwischen wissenschaftlicher Revolution und klassischer Tradition*, Münster: Westfälisches Dampfboot.

Hennessy, R. and Ingraham, C. (eds) (1997) *Materialist Feminism. A Reader in Class, Difference, and Women's Lives*, London: Routledge.

Hepp, A. and Winter, R. (eds) (2003) *Kultur. Medien. Macht. Cultural Studies und Medienanalyse*, Opladen: Westdeutscher Verlag.

Herbert, B. (1993) "In America: The Right Thing," *The New York Times*, October 10, 4/15.

Herbert, S. H. (2000) *Camouflage Isn't Only for Combat: Gender, Sexuality, and Women in the Military*, New York: New York University Press.

Higate, P. (2009) "Private Military Security Companies and the Problem of Men and Masculinities," conference paper, *International Studies Association Conference*, February 15–18, New York.

Higham, S. and Stephens, J. (2004) "Punishment and Amusement," *The Washington Post*, May 22, A01.

Holm, J. (1982) *Women in the Military. An Unfinished Revolution*, Novato, CA: Presidio Press.

Hutchings, K. (2008) "Making Sense of Masculinity and War," *Men and Masculinities*, Vol. 10. No. 4, 389–404.

Iskra, D. (2007) "Attitudes toward Expanding Roles for Navy Women at Sea. Results of a Content Analysis," *Armed Forces & Society*, Vol. 33, No. 2, 203–33.

Iskra, D., Trainor, S., Leithauser, M. and Segal, M. W. (2002) "Women's Participation in Armed Forces Cross-Nationally. Expanding Segal's Model," *Current Sociology*, Vol. 50, No. 5, 771–97.

Janovsky, M. (1997) "Women in the Marines Join the Firing Line," *The New York Times*, April 1, A10.

Janowitz, M. (1965) *Sociology and the Military Establishment*, New York: Sage.

Jay, M. (1984) *Marxism and Totality. The Adventure of a Concept from Lukács to Habermas*. Berkeley, CA: University of California Press.

Jeffords, S. (1989) *The Remasculinization of America. Gender and the Vietnam War*, Bloomington, IN: Indiana University Press.

Jeffords, S. and Rabinovitz, L. (eds) (1994) *Seeing Through the Media, The Persian Gulf War*, New Brunswick, NJ: Rutgers University Press.

Kaldor, M. (1999) *New and Old Wars: Organized Violence in a Global Era*, Cambridge: Polity Press.

Kellner, D. (1995) *Media Culture. Cultural Studies, Identity and the Politics of the Modern and the Postmodern*, London and New York: Routledge.

— (2003) *Media Spectacle*, London and New York: Routledge.

Kleiner, M. S. (2006) *Medien-Heterotopien. Diskursräume einer gesellschaftskritischen Medientheorie*, Bielefeld: Transcript.

Kleykamp, M. (2006) "College, Jobs, or the Military? Enlistment During a Time of War," *Social Science Quarterly*, Vol. 87, No. 2, 272–90.

Kreahling, L. (1997) "In the Service of Their Country: Men and Women in Battle," *The New York Times*, August 10, 13LI8.

Kreisky, E. (1992) "Der Staat als 'Männerbund.' Der Versuch einer feministischen Staatssicht," in E. Biester, B. Geißel, S. Lang, P. Schäfter and B. Young (eds) *Staat aus feministischer Sicht*, Berlin, 53–62.

— (2003) *Fragmente zum Verständnis des Geschlechts des Krieges*. Available at <http://evakreisky.at/onlinetexte/geschlecht_des_krieges.pdf> (accessed 4 December 2009).

— (2008) "Geschwächte Staaten, schwächelnde Männlichkeit und neue Kriege," in W. Sützl and D. Wallnöfer (eds) *Gewalt und Präzision. Krieg und Politik nach Ground Zero*, Wien: Turia & Kant, 137–63.

Kristof, N. (2003) "A Woman's Place," *The New York Times*, April 25, A31.

Laclau, E. and Mouffe, C. (1987) "Post-Marxism Without Apologies," *New Left Review*, Vol. I, No. 166, 79–106.

Lancaster, J. (1992) "Reports of Sexual Assaults Add Fuel To Debate Over Women in Combat," *The Washington Post*, July 14, a.03.

— (1993) "Nearly All Combat Jobs To Be Open to Women. Front-line Ground Units Would Be Excluded," *The Washington Post*, April 29, A1.

Lawrence, W. (1991) "Clearing the Legal Way for Women in Combat," *The Washington Post*, July 28, c.07.

Loeb, V. (2003) "Combat Heroine," *The Washington Post*, November 23, D.01.

Lukács, G. (1923) *Geschichte und Klassenbewusstsein. Studien zur marxistischen Dialektik*, Berlin: Malik.

McCarter, W. M. (2005) "Homo Redneckus. Redefining White Trash in American Culture," *Americana: The Journal of American Popular Culture*, Jan. Available at <http://americanpopularculture.com/style.htm> (accessed April 1, 2005).

McCarthy, C. (1990) "Women at War, a Foolish First," *The Washington Post*, January 14, f.02.

Macur, J. (2005) "In the Line of Fire," *The New York Times*, November 20.

Mann, J. (1991) "The Opportunity of War Service," *The Washington Post*, Febuary 13, d.03.

— (1992) "Who's Not Measuring Up?," *The Washington Post*, July 29, d.23.

Marano, L. (1990) "Arms and the Woman. Would Sexually Mixed U.S. Army Lose Its Wars?," *The Washington Post*, Febuary 18, b.01.

Marcus, R. (2005) "The Woman Warrior," *The Washington Post*, May 24, A.17.

Margolis, M. L. (2000) *True to Her Nature. Changing Advice to American Women*, Florida: Waveland Press.

Mariscal, G. (1991) "In the Wake of the Gulf War. Untying the Yellow Ribbon," *Cultural Critique*, No. 19, 97–117.

Martin, J. (1989) "An Officer and a Lady," *The Washington Post*, March 29, C03.

Marx, K. (1998) "1) ad Feuerbach" (unpublished entry, notebook 1844–7) in *Marx-Engels-Gesamtausgabe*, IV/3, Berlin: Akademie Verlag, 19–21.

— (1962) "Deutsche Ideologie" (unpublished manuscript, 1845) in *Marx-Engels-Werke*, 3, Berlin: Dietz, 13–37.

Masters, Cristina (2009) "Femina Sacra: The 'War on/of Terror,' Women and the Feminine," *Security Dialogue*, Vol. 40, No. 1, 29–49.

Moore, M. (1990a) "Crossing the Culture Gulf. For Female Soldiers, Different Rules," *The Washington Post*, August 23, d.01.

— (1990b) "Women Face Combat Risk. Female GIs Close to Likely Battle Zones," *The Washington Post*, September 12, a.01.

— (1991) "Women on the Battlefield. Gulf War Role Helps Bring Shift in Attitude," *The Washington Post*, June 16, a.01.

Morgan, D. J. J. (1994) "Theater of War. Combat, the Military, and Masculinities," in H. Brod and M. Kaufman (eds) *Theorizing Masculinities*, Thousand Oaks, CA, London and New Delhi: Sage, 165–82.

Moskos, C. (1973) "The Emergent Military. Civil, Traditional, or Plural?," *Pacific Sociological Review*, Vol. 16, No. 2, 255–80.

— (1998) "The Folly of Comparing Race And Gender in the Army," *The Washington Post*, January 4, C.01.

Moskos, C. and Wood, F. (eds) (1988) *The Military: More Than Just a Job?*, Washington: Potomac Books.

Münkler, H. (2005) *The New Wars*, Cambridge: Polity.

— (2006) *Der Wandel des Krieges. Von der Symmetrie zur Asymmetrie*, Weilerswist: Vellbrück Wissenschaft.

Murnane, L. S. (2007) "Legal Impediments to Service. Women in the Military and the Rule of Law," *Duke Journal of Gender Law and Policy*, Vol. 14, Spring, 1061–96.

Murphy, M. F. and Margolis, M. L. (eds) (1995) *Science, Materialism and the Study of Culture*, Gainsville: University Press of Florida.

Myers, S. L. (2003) "A Women Serving on the Blurred Edge of Combat," *The New York Times*, March 19, A16.

National Desk (1993) "Women Warriors," *The New York Times*, April 30, A30.

Neusüß, C. (1985) "Und die Frauen? Tun die denn nichts? Oder: was meine Mutter zu Marx sagt," *beiträge zur feministischen theorie und praxis*, 9-10, 2nd edn, 181–206.

Newitz, A. (1997) "White Savagery and Humiliation: or A New Racial Consciousness in the Media," in A. Newitz and M. Wray (eds) *White Trash: Race and Class in America*, New York and London: Routledge, 131–54.

Niva, S. (1998) "Tough and Tender. New World Order Masculinity and the Gulf War," in M. Zalewski and J. Parpart (eds) *The "Man" Question in International Relations*, Boulder, CO: Westview Press, 109–28.

Nordheimer, J. (1991) "Women's Role in Combat: The War Resumes," *The New York Times*, May 26, 11.

O'Connor, K. (2002) "For Better or for Worse? Women and Women's Rights in the Post 9/11 Climate," in D. Dresang (ed) *American Government in a Changed World: The Effects of September 11, 2001*, New York: Longman, 171–91.

Oliver, K. (2007) *Women as Weapons of War: Iraq, Sex, and the Media*, New York: Columbia University Press.

Oppenheimer, V. K. (1970) *The Female Labor Force in the United States. Demographic and Economic Factors Concerning Its Growth and Changing Composition*, Population Monograph Series, No. 5, Berkeley: Institute of International Studies.

Peach, L. J. (1996) "Gender Ideology in the Ethics of Women in Combat," in J. H. Stiehm (ed.) *It's Our Military, Too. Women and the US Military*, Philadelphia: Temple University Press, 156–94.

Postone, M. (1996) *Time, Labor, and Social Domination. A Reinterpretation of Marx's Critical Theory*, Cambridge: Cambridge University Press.

Poulantzas, N. (1978) *Staatstheorie. Politischer Überbau, Ideologie, Autoritärer Etatismus*, Hamburg: VSA.

Priest, D. (1991a) "Parent Debate Goes Beyond Sex of GI," *The Washington Post*, Febuary 19, a.10.

— (1991b) "Women at the Front, Gulf Role More Diverse Than in Past Wars," *The Washington Post*, March 1, a.01.

— (1997a) "Navy Report Chides Commander For Failing to Bridge Gender Gap. Aviator's Words, Actions Angered Female Carrier Pilots," *The Washington Post*, July 2, a.02.

— (1997b) "Service Group Gave $20,000 To Foe of Women in Combat: Some Female Officers 'Appalled' by Donations," *The Washington Post*, November 8, A.13.

— (1997c) "A Trench Between Women, Jobs," *The Washington Post*, December 28, A.01.

— (1997d) "In a Crunch, Ban on Women Bends," *The Washington Post*, December 30, A.01.

Prokop, D. (2001) *Kampf um die Medien. Geschichtsbuch der neuen kritischen Medienforschung*, Hamburg: VSA.

Quindlen, A. (1992) "Public & Private; Women in Combat," *The New York Times*, January 8, A19.

— (1993) "Public & Private: We're Outta There," *The New York Times*, October 7, Section A29.

Quinn, S. (1991) "Mothers at War. What Are We Doing to Our Kids?," *The Washington Post*, Febuary 10, c.01.

Rayner, R. (1997) "The Warrior Besieged," *The New York Times*, June 22, 6/25.

Reid, T. R. (2003) "Hopi Soldier's Spiritual Return Home," *The Washington Post*, April 7, A19.

Reimann, C. (2000) "Konfliktbearbeitung in Theorie und Praxis. Spielt 'Gender' eine Rolle?," *AFB-Texte*, No. 1.

Reuters (1990) "Confrontation in the Gulf; Saudis Are Dismayed by US Servicewomen," *The New York Times*, August 16, A17.

— (2004) "Ex-Soldier Testifies in Abuse Hearing," *The New York Times*, August 31, A8.

Riche, M. F. (2005) "Demographic Change and Work-force Planning: the All-Volunteer Force," conference paper, *Population Association of America Annual Meeting*, March 31–April 2, Philadelphia.

Ricks, T. and Vogel, S. (2000) "'Killed in Action': Is Gender an Issue?," *The Washington Post*, October 23, A.03.

Robinson, P. (2001) "Operation Restore Hope and the Illusion of a News Media Driven Intervention," *Political Studies*, Vol. 49, 941–56.

Rohter, L. (1993) "Era of Female Pilots Opens with Shrugs and Glee," *The New York Times*, April 29, A1.

Rotberg, R. (2002) "The New Nature of Nation-State Failure," *The Washington Quarterly*, Summer, 85–96.

Ruddick, S. (1982) "Maternal Thinking," *Feminist Studies*, Vol. 6, No. 2, 342–67.

Ruf, W. (2003) *Politische Ökonomie der Gewalt. Staatszerfall und die Privatisierung von Gewalt und Krieg*, Opladen: Leske & Budrich.

Rush, G. (2003) "Jessica Hustled. Porn Mag Pulls Plan to Publish Topless Pics of GI," *The New York Daily News*, 11 November. Available at <http://www.nydailynews.com/front/story/135799p-120870c.html> (accessed February 26, 2004).

Scarborough, R. (2004a) "Pregnant Troops Leave the War," *The Washington Times*, June 16, A01.

— (2004b) "Zarqawi Targets Female Soldier," *The Washington Times*, July 1, A01.

Schlichte, K. (2002) "Neues über den Krieg. Einige Anmerkungen zum Stand der Kriegsforschung in den Internationalen Beziehungen," *Zeitschrift für Internationale Beziehungen*, Vol. 9, No. 1, 113–38.

— (2004) "Neue Kriege und alte Thesen? Wirklichkeit und Repräsentation kriegerischer Gewalt in der Politikwissenschaft," conference paper, *Neue Kriegstheorien. eine Zwischenbilanz,* March 25–27, Frankfurt/Main.

Schmitt, E. (1991a) "Head of Army Sees Chance of Female Fliers in Combat," *The New York Times*, June 2, 132.

— (1991b) "Ban on Women in Combat Divides Four Service Chiefs," *The New York Times*, June 19, A16.

— (1991c) "Senate Votes to Remove Ban On Women as Combat Pilots," *The New York Times*, August 1, A1.

— (1992) "The Military Has a Lot To Learn About Women," *The New York Times*, August 2, 43.

— (1993) "The Nation: Reaching the Stars in the New Military," *The New York Times*, September 4, 4/5.

— (1994a) "Aspin Moves to Open Many Military Jobs to Women," *The New York Times*, January 14, A22.

— (1994b) "Pilot's Death Renews Debate Over Women in Combat Roles," *The New York Times*, October 30.

— (1996) "Role of Women in the Military Is Again Bringing Debate," *The New York Times*, December 29, 114.

Schultz, S. and Yeung, C. (2005) *Private Military Security Companies and Gender*, Report for the Geneva Centre for the Democratic Control of Armed Forces (DCAF: component of Gender and SSR toolkit, tool 10).

Sciolino, E. (1990) "Battle Lines Are Shifting on Women in War," *The New York Times*, January 25, A1.

— (1992) "Female POW Is Abused, Kindling Debate," *The New York Times*, 29 June, A1.

Scott Tyson, A. (2005a) "Panel Votes to Ban Women From Combat," *The Washington Post*, May 12, A.08.

— (2005b) "For Female GIs, Combat Is a Fact," *The Washington Post*, May 13, A.01.

— (2005c) "More Objections to Women-in-Combat Ban," *The Washington Post*, May 18, A.05.

— (2005d) "Amendment Targets Role of Female Troops," *The Washington Post*, May 19, A.04.

— (2005e) "Bid to Limit Women in Combat Withdrawn," *The Washington Post*, May 26, A.01.

Segal, D. and Segal, M. W. (1983) "Change in Military Organization," *Annual Review of Sociology*, Vol. 9, 151–70.

— (2004) "America's Military Population," *Population Bulletin*, Vol. 59, No. 4, 1–40.

Segal, M. W. (1986) "The Military and the Family As Greedy Institutions," *Armed Forces & Society*, Vol. 13, No. 1, 9–38.

— (1995) "Women's Military Roles Cross-Nationally. Past, Present, and Future," *Gender and Society*, Vol. 9, No. 6, 757–75.

— (1999) "Gender and the Military," in J. S. Chafetz (ed) *Handbook of the Sociology of Gender*, New York: Kluwer Academic/Plenum, 563–81.

Segal, M. W., Segal, D., Bachman, J., Freedman-Doan, P. and O'Malley, P. (1998) "Gender and the Propensity to Enlist in the US Military," *Gender Issues*, Vol. 16, No. 3, 65–87.

Seifert, R. (1995) "Destruktive Konstruktionen. Ein Beitrag zur Dekonstruktion des Verhältnisses von Militär, Nation und Geschlecht," in E. Haas (ed.) *Verwirrung der Geschlechter. Dekonstruktion und Feminismus*, Munic–Vienna: Profil, 157–86.

— (1996) *Militär. Kultur. Identität: Individualisierung, Geschlechterverhältnisse und die soziale Konstruktion des Soldaten*, Bremen: Temmen.

Shanker, T. (2005) "House Bill Would Preserve, and Limit the Role of Women in Combat Zones," *The New York Times*, May 20, A20.

Shenon, P. (1991) "At Combat's Doorstep, She Confronts Peril and Male Doubt," *The New York Times*, Febuary 24, 116.

— (1997) "Army Official Creates Furor Calling Marines 'Extremists'", *The New York Times*, November 14, A30.

Sheridan, M. B. (2003) "In This Woman's Army, Combat Now Part of the Duty," *The Washington Post*, March 15, A.01.

Simmons, Deborah (2004) "Un-American Activities," *The Washington Times*, May 6, A21.

Sjoberg, L. (2010) (ed.) *Gender and International Security: Feminist Perspectives*, London: Routledge.

Sjoberg, L. and Gentry, C. E. (2008) "Reduced to Bad Sex: Narratives of Violent Women from the Bible to the War on Terror," *International Relations*, Vol. 22, No. 1, 5–23.

Stabile, C. A. and Kumar, D. (2005) "Unveiling Imperialism: Media, Gender and the War in Afghanistan," *Media, Culture & Society*, Vol. 27, No. 5, 765–82.

Stachowitsch, S. (2008) "Von Heldinnen und Monstern. Personalisierung und Vergeschlechtlichung von Kriegsnarrativen an den Beispielen Jessica Lynch und Lynndie England," in W. Sützl and D. Wallnöfer, Doris (eds) *Gewalt und Präzision. Krieg und Politik nach Ground Zero*, Vienna: Turia & Kant, 165–86.

Starr, H. (2011) *Dealing With Failed States: Crossing Analytical Boundaries*, London: Routledge.

Stevenson, R. W. (2004) "Abuse Scandal: The Aftershocks," *The New York Times*, May 9, 4/2.

Stiehm, J. (1988) "The Effects of Myths about Military Women on the Waging of War," in E. Isaksson (ed.) *Women and the Military System*, New York: St Martin's Press.

— (1989) *Arms and the Enlisted Woman*, Philadelphia: Temple University Press.

— (1996) (ed.) *It's Our Military, Too. Women and the US Military*, Philadelphia: Temple University Press, 205–19.

Sullivan, J. (1991) "Army Pilot's Death Stuns Her New Jersey Neighbors," *The New York Times*, March 7, B1.

Thomas, P. J. (1978) "Women in the Military: America and the British Commonwealth: Historical Similarities," *Armed Forces & Society*, Vol. 4, No. 4, 623–46.

Tickner, J. A. (1992) *Gender in International Relations. Feminist Perspectives in Achieving Global Security*, New York: Columbia University Press.

— (2001) *Gendering World Politics. Issues and Approaches in the Post-Cold War Era*, New York: Columbia University Press.

— (2002) "Feminist Perspectives on 9/11," *International Studies Perspectives*, Vol. 3, No. 4, 333–50.

Titunik, R. (2000) "The First Wave. Gender Integration and Military Culture," *Armed Forces & Society*, Vol. 26, No. 2, 229–57.

— (2008) "The Myth of the Macho Military," *Polity*, Vol. 40, No. 2, 137–63.

Tyler May, E. (1991) "Women in the Wild Blue Yonder," *The New York Times*, August 7, A21.

Van Creveld, M. (2000) "The Great Illusion: Women in the Military," *Millennium. Journal of International Studies*, Vol. 29, No. 2, 429–42.

Vobejda, B. and Health, T. (1993) "Combat Role for Women Seen Likely to Have Wider Social Impact," *The Washington Post*, April 29, A.06.

Vogt, D., Bruce, T. A., Street, A. E. and Stafford, J. (2007) "Attitudes Toward Women and Tolerance for Sexual Harassment Among Reservists," *Violence Against Women*, Vol. 13, No. 9, 879–900.

Warner, J. and Asch, B. (2001) "The Record and Prospects of the All-Volunteer Military in the United States," *The Journal of Economic Perspectives*, Vol. 15, No. 2, 169–92.

Weber, M. (1922) *Wirtschaft und Gesellschaft*, Tübingen: Mohr.

Wheeler, J. (2004) "Take It Like a Man," *The Washington Times*, 20 May. Available at <http://www.washingtontimes.com/op-ed/20040520-083647-9853r.htm> (accessed July 29, 2004).

Wiegman, R. (1994) "Missiles and Melodrama. Masculinity and the Televisual War," in S. Jeffords and L. Rabinovitz (eds) *Seeing Through the Media. The Persian Gulf War*, New Brunswick: Rutgers University Press, 171–87.

Wilgoren, J. (2003) "A New War Brings New Role For Women," *The New York Times*, March 28, B1.

Williams, R. (1980) *Problems in Materialism and Culture. Selected Essays*, London: Verso.

Williams, R. (2005) "Women Rising to Higher Positions in the Military," in *American Armed Forces Press Service*, April 3, 1–2.

Williamson, E. (2004a) "One Soldier's Unlikely Act," *The Washington Post*, May 6, A16.

— (2004b) "Prisoner Abuse Scandal Brings 27 Seconds of Fame to Soldier's Relatives," *The Washington Post*, May 9, C04.

— (2004c) "Witness to Abuse to Be Heard," *The Washington Post*, 20 August, A12.

Wodak, R. (2001) "The Discourse-historical Approach," in R. Wodak and M. Meyer (eds) *Methods of Critical Discourse Analysis*, London: Sage, 63–94.

WREI (Women's Research and Education Institute) (no date) *Chronology of Significant Legal and Policy Changes Affecting Women in the Military: 1947–2003*. Available at <http://www.wrei.org/Women%20in%20the%20Military/Women%20in%20the%20Military%20Chronology%20of%20Legal%20Policy.pdf> (accessed June 26, 2009).

Young, I. M. (2003) "The Logic of Masculinist Protection: Reflections on the Current Security State," *Signs: Journal of Women in Culture and Society*, Vol. 29, No. I, 1–25.

Yuval-Davis, N. (1997) *Gender and Nation*, London: Sage.

Zalewski M. and Parpart, J. (eds) (1998) *The "Man" Question in International Relations*, Boulder, CO: Westview Press.

Zernike, K. (2004) "Prison Guard Calls Abuse Routine and Sometimes Amusing," *The New York Times*, May 16, 1/1.Index: Saskia Stachowitsch "Gender and Military Labor Markets in the US"

Index